Puget Sound Lumberjack

Wilfred Nevue

with
Susan M. Branting

Ten Sleep Press
Columbia, Maryland

Puget Sound Lumberjack

ISBN 978-0-9859812-1-1

Table of Contents

Wilfred Nevue, second from right, at the end of a skidroad. (From the author's collection.)

Introduction

I FIRST SAW LAND DEVASTATED BY LOGGING when visiting Puget Sound in the mid 1980s. My husband and I, driving along blue highways, exclaimed in surprise at the big patches of ugly land littered with the detritus of denuded forests. Dark pine trees crowded the edges of these meadows that had once been thick with Douglas fir, spruce, cedar, and hemlock. Now there were only masses of severed limbs and old stumps, dense and tangled.

This is the land Wilfred Nevue worked during the early part of the 20th Century. He had helped to cut the last of the great white pines in the Upper Peninsula of Michigan and he came to Puget Sound to earn money for college. He knew that working as a lumberjack was destroying these beautiful trees, but he was a man of his era and this was a job he thought he knew.

Wilfred Nevue was my grandfather. I knew little about him when I was growing up. My mother, Eileen, who was his second child, rarely spoke of him, and because my father was in the Air Force, we traveled far from Richmond, Indiana, where he lived. He died in 1966, when I was sixteen and living in Germany. I remember meeting him just three times.

It was not until my mother passed away in 2011 and I inherited newspaper clippings, daguerreotypes, letters, manuscripts, and a stack of photographs of logging activities that I began to explore his life.

He was born in 1886 in Champion, in the Upper Peninsula of Michigan, the child of a hasty marriage. His father disappeared when he was six months old, and his mother was institutionalized when he was four for mental health problems and died when she was in her late 20s. He was raised on a farm by his grandmother and her second husband, who was her first husband's brother.

While his relationship with his grandmother was deep, he had difficulty getting along with his great uncle (whom he called "grandfather") and with her children, his uncles and aunts. After graduating from high school, he left home to earn money for college, an ambition beyond the aspirations of the rest of his family. At this point, he turned to logging.

Among the objects I inherited were two manuscripts, one on logging in the Huron Mountain region and another on growing up on a farm. The first is dense with facts about timber products and logging methods and would probably be of interest only to logging historians. The second manuscript, "A Boy's Paradise," I edited and turned into a book, *A Boy's Paradise: Life on a Turn-of-the-Century Farm in the Upper Peninsula of Michigan.*

Wilfred had published pieces of these manuscripts, particularly "A Boy's Paradise," in magazines and newspapers.

Some of these articles I discovered when I searched for his name on the web; it turned up a surprising number of times. And I stumbled across something else — a third manuscript in a historical museum's archives in Washington State: "Puget Sound Lumberjack."

Like his original "A Boy's Paradise," the text of "Puget Sound Lumberjack" tends toward the overwrought and overwritten. It's also full of details that might fascinate lumberjacks and logging historians but that read dryly for the uninitiated. Nevertheless, the manuscript is rich with anecdotes and insights into life in the early 20th century. I have tried to retain the content I think will be of interest to a general readership while including some idea of the complex, grueling work of logging on Puget Sound. This means that I have taken out chunks of text on the diameter of cables and how such equipment as loading-hooks, luffs, and road sheaves were used. I have omitted entirely a chapter on bucking and another on how the last horses were used in logging in 1907. For those who wish fuller details, the original manuscript can be found online in the HathiTrust Digital Library (hathitrust.org).

Included in my inherited trove were photographs my grandfather intended to accompany "Puget Sound Lumberjack" but which are missing from the online version. Photographers visited lumber camps and sold the pictures they took to the companies and workers. Wilfred collected a nice sampling, which are labeled here, "From the author's collection." Unless otherwise indicated, all other photos were gathered for illustration purposes from WikiMedia Commons and are copyright free.

Susan M. Branting

Columbia, MD

February 2021

CHAPTER 1

My Adventure Begins

A LL OF MY LIFE I HAD LIVED in a primarily-lumberjack environment around Champion in Marquette County in the Upper Peninsula of Michigan. My grandfather, with whom I lived, was a small farmer and a lumberjack. The other men of our household, our nearest neighbors, and many of the men in town were also of that occupation.

Our home was near the logging camps, and as soon as I was old enough to go into the woods alone, I went to the nearby camps on weekends. In my first year of high school, I ran off and worked part of the winter of 1901–02 in Wisconsin. During the winter of 1904–05, I worked in the Upper Peninsula on a tributary of the Peshekee River, and in the spring of 1905, I drove logs on that river.

While in a camp in Minnesota, during the winter of 1905–06, I heard talk of logging on Puget Sound and of the good wages that were paid there. As soon as logging stopped in early March 1906, I headed to Minneapolis and shipped out with a trainload of laborers and a few lumberjacks.

Each man had paid two dollars to an employment agency

to work on a railroad extension that was being constructed along the bank of the Columbia River from Kennewick, Washington, to Portland, Oregon. To encourage workers to go west, the cost of a ticket was nominal, though the railroad made sure the return fair was not.

During our several days of travel westward, the men were companionable, and it became clear that not one of the gang intended to work at railroad construction. They remained on the train until it reached Spokane. After that, whenever the train stopped, some of the fellows got off for good. By the time the train arrived at Kennewick there were only two of us left, and we decided to go on to Seattle.

We reached Seattle late in the evening of March 17, 1906, while the city was enveloped in one of those mists for which Puget Sound is so well known.

I had arrived in the country of the Douglas fir.

CHAPTER 2

From Canthook to Skidroad

THE RAILROAD PASSENGER STATION in Seattle was an inadequate structure for a port city of that size.[1] The station was located on and parallel to the waterfront on Elliott Bay.[2] Along the waterfront were a long row of piers, shipping docks of all sizes and importance, and ship-building yards, as well as fish markets and sawmills at each end.

On the other side of the station was a long, narrow area of dirty, dodgy, vault-like, secondhand stores and dungeon-like pawnshops, each with its cluster of three gilded balls hanging above the sidewalk. There were many slummy saloons with calk-frayed floors and stinky free lunches of salt herring and stale, moldy bread in open dishes. Obscene pictures of women decorated the walls. Cockroaches, fleas, and lice infested the flophouses and joints. Restaurants displayed good menus behind little windows — menus that were frauds when one stepped inside. Large, gaudy illustrated posters advertised

---

[1] *Seattle's estimated population in 1906 was 943,167. Wright, Carrol D. The New Century Book of Facts, 459. Springfield, Mass.: King-Richardson Company, 1909.*
[2] *This station was on Railroad Avenue (today called Alaskan Way) and was replaced later that year by the King Street Station.*

venereal disease museums and clinics that preyed on lumber-jacks, sawmill workers, dock wallopers, sailors, drifters, the elite, and the gullible along the Skid Road. Procurers strolled the entire route openly and brazenly pandering with cards and handbills for the ladies in the cribs on King Street. Nearest to the station were small employment offices of all degrees of integrity.

Early the next morning I sought out the employment offices along the waterfront. The mist hung thick and sticky. The air reeked of rotting fish, latrine stench from saloons, and accumulated filth.

As I zigzagged among fog-shrouded figures, I saw that the employment offices were open for business. Under pale, yellowish lights, barkers and solicitors competed vigorously for the attention of small groups of men huddled nearby. Job-seekers, loafers, and moochers shuffled about reading the colored cards tacked to the walls inside and outside of the offices. Some moved their heads as if they were reading, then asked questions. They were nearly all illiterate. Others mumbled or stood silently. The scene depressed but did not deter me.

I sought a job as a canthooker[3] or teamster, jobs I had held in Michigan and Minnesota. I would show these lumberjacks how to skid logs with a team of horses, how to whirl a canthook to cut a rolling log as it went up the skids. But I heard men talk-

---

[3] *A lumberjack who moves logs using a canthook, a tool consisting of a long, wooden handle and an iron hook.*

ing only about jobs that were entirely unknown to me.

"Don't you want canthook men?" I asked an agent in a low voice.

He guffawed. "Say, brother, no use for canthook men around here. This is timber, not toothpicks." He looked around for approval and added, "Just from the east, eh?"

I grimaced and withdrew, then loitered to regain my courage. Two men grinned in my direction and nudged each other. I slunk to another office where a small gathering stood scanning the posters and talking about jobs. Their low conversation revealed them to be sailors, sawmill men, salmon fishermen from the north, and railroad construction laborers. Several spoke foreign languages. All of them had come to Seattle to spend their stakes, and they had apparently done well.

The lumberjacks were easy to spot. They wore calked shoes, blue woolen shirts, and stagged overalls[4] or stiff brown pants. I was cleaner than the men around me and better dressed — and sober. They had come from their jobs on the Pacific coast. I had come from another region, and I was conscious of being conspicuous. If I ventured a question about logging, the response was a grin accompanied with some slighting remark, usually, "Just from the east, eh?" and then, "Just another scissorbill."[5] Some stared at me suspiciously. One handed me a quack doctor's card as he looked down the front of my pants suggestively.

---

[4] *Overalls or pants shortened by being roughly cut off at the hem.*
[5] *A showoff, an eastern lumberjack; generally, a stupid person.*

I walked along the long row of employment offices, stopping at every one, then sauntered over the tracks to the docks and back up the side street leading to the city's business section, hoping that there were better employment offices somewhere, but they were all near the railroad tracks.

In the windows and doors of the stores, hotels, and saloons removed from the tracks were neat signs: "No Calk Shoes Allowed." Men seldom wore calked shoes in Minneapolis, Duluth, or Marquette, and then only in the spring.

But in Seattle and anywhere on the coast, I was told, lumberjacks wore calked shoes year-round. One could not work without them. How strange, I thought. I had rubbers, for cold and snow. As I would soon find out, rubbers were ill suited for mud and the scorching days of summer and did not work in big timber or on mountain slopes.

Back along the tracks, I scanned the display boards and walls. Lumberjacks were in high demand. Frequently, the name of the logging companies, the wages, and the location of the camps were omitted. The lumberjacks discussed — and cussed — the loggers. Each company was judged by the pay and the food, as well as the distance from Seattle, Tacoma, Everett, Bellingham, and Aberdeen (Portland was too far away). Those cities had the best attractions for lumberjacks, and Pacific Coast lumberjacks were generally single and unattached — they were nearly all floaters.

The employment agents conducted their businesses with

the same degree of integrity as men in any business — some were honest and some were rascals. I was told that some employment agents were patronized by the less competent men, while others dealt only with skilled workmen, and they paid good wages to get them. The dishonest agents invariably were the ones who put out the signs with only the jobs listed, with the names of the employers revealed only after an applicant stepped inside. Such employment agencies were in collusion with the unscrupulous camp foremen with whom they split the fees. In those camps during periods of slack employment, lumberjacks were hired (usually one at a time), then after working one or two days, they were fired. Frequently, there were no jobs — only the graft. The forests suffered from the inefficient labor and management. But who cared? There was lots of timber. The future be damned.

So, I read the signs that I did not understand. Logging was the only work where good wages were payed. And if I stayed in camp rather than caroused in Seattle, I could save my earnings. I wanted to go to college.

I had seen some big trees from the train, and they fascinated me. So, I listened to the barkers and heard their rotten, obscene remarks about the ladies of King Street. But I had not yet seen Seattle — Seattle with its beautiful streets and theaters, its great public library, and the busy public market overlooking Elliott Bay. Seattle of Queen Ann Hill, Lake Washington, Green Lake, and the University of Washington with its great buildings, which had been built among the firs and stumps and deadfalls and brush — the stumps and deadfalls where later I sat and breathed in the atmosphere of refinement, education, and inspiration.

But that was the future. Now I had to sort through signs and cards of many colors advertising jobs that I knew nothing about: hooktender; chokerman; dogger; engineers for yard donkeys, road donkeys and other "donkeys"; signalpunk; rigging-slinger; sniper; skidroad foreman; and others.

The only familiar jobs were those of railroad sectionman and swamper, but upon inquiry I was told that skidroad building was also common labor. If there had been any likeness between Puget Sound logging and eastern logging, I would have tried my luck at one of the strange jobs, but I could see none.

After a forenoon of indecision and inquiry among the offices, I pompously walked into one of the more attractive offices and bluntly accepted a job building skidroads for McDougal & Jackson, contractors for the St. Paul & Tacoma Lumber Company, whose camp was four miles up a mountain near Buckley. I paid the two-dollar fee and got my little yellow ticket and directions to Buckley.

The agent grinned, "Good luck," he said. "Don't break too many canthooks."

CHAPTER 3

A Night at Buckley

T HAT AFTERNOON, I VISITED BUCKLEY, a village in Pierce County, about thirty miles from Tacoma. Buckley had a small church with an oversized steeple (whose pastor, I would later find, occasionally preached in camps without making much impression), a state bank, a little smutty hotel — The Grand — and abundant saloons. Scattered, but clinging to Buckley, was a fine element of people who were clearing acre ranches from cutover land and who worked in the sawmill of the Page Lumber Company. But Buckley proper was small and concentrated; it was a logging and sawmill town first.

That evening, I learned many things about Puget Sound that were surprisingly foreign to me and my experiences in northern Michigan. It rained thirteen months a year, the fellows claimed, so if I expected to work as a lumberjack, I would have to do it in the rain — and mud and slush. As I stood around kibitzing blackjack games and engaged in conversation with fellows who wanted to borrow a dollar or mooch a drink, I learned much more. The boys were nice — and solicitous. Foolishly, I told them I was green about Puget Sound logging ways, so they kidded me about horses and canthooks. I paid attention to their jibes to help me prepare for what was to come.

Most of these lumberjacks were employees of McDougal & Jackson and were broke and headed to their camps. Generally, lumberjacks did not go to camp with money. Saloons, gambling, and prostitutes had strangle holds on them — whiskey and the ladies, "Tom, Dick, and Harry," and Old Maud in the little red house down by the railroad bridge, or the independent ones upstairs over the saloons.

That night I went to bed late. The bartenders, with an eye for business, announced the saloons were open all night. I rented a bed in a room at The Grand, which had a number of beds in each room for lumberjacks. I did not sleep much. Bedbugs, fleas and roaches cavorted.

At that time, I had a considerable amount of money on me — about forty dollars — from my Minnesota winter earnings, but I appeared broke, or tried to. Lumberjacks were not known for hanging onto their money when it could be spent. Keeping one's hand on one's pocket was an indication of unspent cash. However, during the nearly five years I worked on Puget Sound, I never heard of a lumberjack stealing another lumberjack's money. There was a sense of honor among them, or maybe it was fear, for lumberjacks moved about a lot and they might meet again. In camp, I looked prosperous, and when the fellows learned that I was saving money to go to college, they were sometimes encouraging, but nevertheless skeptical. Frequently they jibed, "Well, Bill [their nickname for me], when you going to college?" Occasionally some of them tried to borrow money from me after they struck town.

McDougal & Jackson's Camp 4, I was told, was four miles up a logging road on a mountain. The logging train would pull in at about ten o'clock in the forenoon. The railroad belonged to the camp outfit, and there was no schedule for its one train.

The mountain climber and six loaded flatcars on the siding at Buckley, 1906. (From the author's collection.)

The next morning, I rose early and prepared to wait for the train that would take me to camp. The Oregon mist[6] cleared rather rapidly — summer was nearing — and by ten o'clock the sun was breaking through the clouds. Still, the location of the camp as pointed out to me was indistinct on the mountain side.

While waiting, I strolled to the sidetrack where several flatcars were loaded with the largest and longest logs I had ever seen, ready to be hauled to the mill of The St. Paul & Tacoma Lumber Company in Tacoma. Just three or four logs filled each

---

[6] *A term for a heavy mist, associated with Oregon but also used in Washington.*

car and certain features about them interested me intensely. The bark was sliced off along the entire length of one side of each log and the edge around one end was rounded off. More than ever, I was anxious to be in camp.

After walking along each side of the string of cars and laboriously climbing to the top of one and posing to my satisfaction (and wishing that I had a picture of myself there to send to my folks), I returned to the business area of Buckley, had breakfast, and loitered about. At nine o'clock I went to the little bank to deposit my savings. I would soon begin to build on the deposit.

I was glad to get to the bank, because on the street, though I tried to appear broke, I felt obligated to buy several moochers twenty-five-cent meals and drinks. I would have to work with these fellows.

The cashier, who was the entire bank staff, was at the door when I reached it. He and I soon engaged in general conversation during which he asked me what I did. I told him that I was going to work on the skidroads for McDougal & Jackson, and when he learned that I wished to deposit money instead of cashing a check, he warmed up to me. I expected him to smile and jibe a bit and say, "Just from the east, eh?" But he did not. I must have impressed him with my sincerity because his attitude became more and more friendly. Lumberjacks were not depositors in banks — they were check-cashers — and the little banks and the saloons nearly always charged one or two percent for cashing checks. That was how they thrived.

After depositing my money, I returned to the sidetrack to wait for the log train. I watched smoke from the engine weave a meandering course over the forest that began at the edge of the valley. The train swung and curved among the trees until suddenly, as though being ejected out of a great cut, it slid into the open valley and coasted to the siding. The loaded cars were readily pushed onto the sidetrack and empty ones were pulled into place, ready to be hauled up the mountain to the camp landing.

CHAPTER 4

Journey Toward Destruction

THE LOCOMOTIVE ON MCDOUGAL & JACKSON'S logging railroad thoroughly aroused my curiosity. It was a queer-looking piece of machinery. Except for the flute-shaped smokestack, there was not a feature about it that resembled anything that I had ever seen, even in pictures. The boiler was noticeably stubby, the engine and the tender were on the same steel frame, and the driving mechanism extended under the sides of the entire length of both. The locomotive was manufactured by the Lima Locomotive Works.[7]

Conspicuous was the absence of large drivewheels like those on common locomotives. All the drivewheels were uniform and small, like those under the cowcatcher of regular engines. The four cylinders, two on each side, were small upright against the boiler. The pistons functioned vertically like those of an automobile motor. They were fastened to long shafts that turned the drivewheels by means of gear connections. When the locomotive was running, it made a burring sound. In prin-

---

[7] *The company is best known for producing the Shay locomotive, which was geared down to provide more of the pulling ability needed for heavy loads on steep grades.*

ciple and construction, and in the operation of its mechanism, that mountain climber was similar to a gas engine.

The fireman told me that the locomotive's greatest speed was about eight miles an hour; however, it could pull several loaded flatcars up a grade not negotiable by any of the engines with which I was familiar. There was no airbrake equipment. Instead, while the train descended a grade, the brakeman balanced along the logs and jumped from car to car to set the hand brakes. Sometimes the fireman helped.

The locomotive burned wood. Two cutters worked along the track, sawing and splitting fir into two-foot-long pieces from dry snags, poor-quality wood, and logs that had rolled off of the cars. Fir was the only wood suitable for fuel. The thick bark and the pitchy snags were dry and made intense fire.

The train had neither a turntable nor a turn-around track at either end of the line. The locomotive just went back and forth and did equally well in both directions.

At Buckley, I watched the locomotive push its loaded cars onto the sidetrack, then couple to a string of six empty flatcars. It backed to a small open platform, and the brakeman and the fireman loaded provisions and camp supplies, including a large reel of three-fourth-inch Roebling steel cable.[8] After everything was loaded, we started for camp.

I was curious about that reel of cable because the label in-

---

[8] *John Augustus Roebling was a German-born American civil engineer who designed and built wire rope suspension bridges, most famously the Brooklyn Bridge.*

dicated that there were two thousand feet of it. What could that thing be for in a logging camp?

Thoroughly aware of my ignorance about Puget Sound logging, I just sat on the reel as it lay flat and kept my mouth shut.

Another lumberjack climbed onto the same flatcar. He was a Swede. That was obvious — he was blond, and he spoke in the singsong accent characteristic of the people of that nationality. I was certain that he was a Swede for I knew many of those fine people in my native Upper Peninsula of Michigan. The man wore calked shoes and the indispensable blue flannel shirt. He toted a small canvas sack, which we called a turkey back east and that was commonly used by lumberjacks, and two woolen blankets rolled into a bundle. The sack and bundle were tied together and carried over the shoulder by passing an arm through a loop made of clothesline. In contrast, I had a new suitcase with some useless clothes, including my rubber boots that I had already concluded were obsolete. However, what was most curious were the blankets. I had none.

My fellow lumberjack was red and puffy-eyed from carousing, and he soon fell asleep. His head swayed. Several times he jerked and slumped to fall. But the air was cool and invigorating, so he straightened and bobbed, straightened and bobbed, until he raised his head a bit and mumbled. Then more mumbling. Finally, we fell into conversation.

He told me what to look for in logging camps and which

jobs paid best. He also told me how long he had been in this country and that he expected to return to his dear Sweden one day after he had saved enough money.

His name was Ole. Nearly all Swedes were named Ole. If their names were not Ole, they were nicknamed Ole anyway. A Swede was an Ole.

Ole's head kept drooping toward the floor of the car as I enjoyed the grandeur of the country and forest. We exchanged short reminiscences. I told Ole a little of what I had done and where I had just come from, and that I proposed to save money to attend the University of Michigan. I could not keep my mouth shut about that! He tilted his eyebrows up and chuckled a bit. Then, laboriously raising his stupored head, he sleepily looked at me with those festering eyes with little beads of puss in the corners, and said, "No, no, you won't. Jacks don't do that. You'll forget it. Once a fella's a lum'jack in these camps, he never gets out. He can't." Then Ole mentioned the University of Uppsala and how he had missed going. One day he would go back to that university.

But Ole's mind was unstable. He changed his plans as we went along. He might not go to Sweden after all. He might buy some cutover land, a ranch of two acres or so, down in Puyallup Valley. Or maybe some of that stump ground through which we had just passed on our way out of Buckley. Looked pretty good. He would raise hops on tall poles, not like those hop poles around Puyallup. "Ever pick hops?"

"No, I never picked hops," I said.

"Lots of Indian girls at hop picking. Better than the Seattle girls," Ole said. "Ever been on King Street?"

"Were those hop poles down around Puyallup?" I asked. "Thought they were bean poles."

Ole laughed.

And he would raise strawberries and other good things and sell them at the market in Seattle.

"Ever go to the Seattle market? Up on the hill toward Ballard?" he asked. "On the other side of the city from King Street."

"No," I said.

"Christ you're ignorant," Ole said.

And he would have chickens. Nice big ones, those big gray ones. "Whatdya call 'em?" Ole asked. Oh yes, and a milk cow. Plenty of fresh milk. That was better than whiskey.

I nodded.

"Yes, sir, I'll quit drinking," Ole said. "This is my last spree." He smiled in a grimace. "And I'll send for my girl in Sweden."

He opened his turkey and fumbled for his girl's picture. When he couldn't find it, he pulled out a bottle of whiskey instead, a large, brown bottle with a fancy label — Old Crow or Three Star Hennessy. He stroked its sides fondly and slid its neck through his quivering hands. He took a lingering drink, blinked, shook his head and puckered his lips. He sucked the tips of his thin yellow mustache and wiped his mouth with the back of his hand. When he raised the bottle toward his mouth, he noticed that I was looking at him expectantly and handed me the bottle. That was good whiskey to sober lips, warming whiskey in that damp and cool mountain air — in that Oregon mist on that March day.

"What are those for?" I asked, pointing at the blankets. In the logging camps of the Lake Superior region, lumberjacks did not carry blankets. Employers furnished them, and lumberjacks slept in pairs. The blankets were lousy before spring, I told Ole.

"But not out here," Ole replied.

I soon learned much about that, too. Each lumberjack provided his own blankets and slept alone. Without blankets, he was cold — and the nights were cold the year round in the mountains, especially during the Oregon mist season, which was most of the year. If a lumberjack slept in dirty bedding that was his affair. But he must not be lousy — he must not be a cootie — that was everybody's affair. When Ole mentioned cooties, I felt a bit of itching on the back of my neck, a live bit of Minnesota had come along.

Ole changed the subject. "I'm going to buck," he said, "That pays pretty good, two-fifty a day."

I was to be paid two dollars and twenty-five cents a day on the skidroad. That twenty-five cents was a significant difference. Board was three dollars and fifty cents a week. Nonetheless, these were good wages.

"What's bucking?" I asked.

"Oh, that's bucking logs alone," he said, "Sawing felled trees into logs alone."

Ole described the various operations that were necessary for good bucking. How easy bucking was when the trees lay just right and did not contain too much pitch. But the fallers[9] did not always care how a big fir fell, and they did not carefully mark them for convenient bucking.

"Damn some of those fallers!" Ole said.

Fallers and buckers. How little I knew.

Ole explained how he could saw from on top of a trunk and prevent the logs from splitting, and also how he sawed upward from under the log when the cut could not be kept open with wedges. He showed me a little iron wheel — a bedstead caster with a groove in which the back of the saw moved smoothly when he sawed upward. I did not know anything about bucking logs. In contrast to those buckers, a good eastern sawyer was a rank novice, a punk,[10] a scissorbill.

The train continued its climb, burring hard. Wood ash and tiny sparks sifted out of the spark-arrester, and the flanges of the wheels ground along the continuous curves of the railroad. The engine stopped several times to take on fuel. The brakeman, the fireman, and the engineer jumped off to throw wood into the tender. Once, the water tank was filled from a long hose

---

[9] *The lumberjacks who cut down the trees.*
[10] *A young man.*

connected to an open wooden tank on the hillside. Another time the engine stopped so that we could drink from a particularly clear and cool stream.

Ole was very thirsty. He was sobering up, so as we went up the mountain side, he became more and more talkative. He talked less about Sweden, his mother, his sweetheart, and the ranch. He shifted to other subjects, particularly those ladies of Skid Road, King Street, and Tacoma's A Street. He had not yet heard of Tom, Dick, and Harry, nor old of Maud in the little red house by the bridge.

Ole sipped from the bottle, which was becoming empty. He held the bottle up to look through the glass, but he did not pass it. He licked the wet label, then fondly slid the bottle into his turkey.

During that first morning riding from Buckley to Camp 4, I saw something that inspired me with its beauty. I had seen the great forests of the Huron Mountains in Michigan, but they were insignificant in comparison. This was one of the world's grandest panoramas of beautiful forests.

I saw the beginning of its destruction. From the village of Buckley, the vastness of the region had the appearance of a continuous primeval forest. One could not see the scars in it. The long, gradual slopes to the timber line on the mountains looked like a vast, dark-green canopy. Only the snowcaps of the Olympic and the Cascade mountains were bare of timber, and snow-crowned Mt. Rainier to the southeast stood guard over the entire region. The forests seemed limitless.

At first, as we left Buckley, the train passed for some distance over the flat-bottomed valley that was rapidly being cleared of stumps to make ranches around many new homes. On Puget Sound, every parcel of ground, no matter how small, was a ranch. The panorama shrank quickly as we approached the edge of the valley, but the trees took form and became more distinguishable. Then the train plunged head-on into the forest.

There, as the train climbed up the mountain, towered the tall, straight, and beautiful brown-trunk trees, so near I could almost touch them. I had heard about these trees inadequately and vaguely from the lumberjacks in Minnesota.

To my left on the long, high ridge, to my right in the deep valley, and ahead, far, far up to the snow caps of the mountains, was timber. Behind, down to the narrow White River Valley and beyond were forests. Oh, those big brown trunks standing on an endless carpet of tall ferns and small bushes!

We climbed and climbed. As we penetrated deeper, the green began to dull, and ahead was the bright blue of the sky. We were above the fog and clouds, a gradual shift at first, then a more rapid change. The brown trunks were grayer, the ground was turning black, and the ferns grew yellower and thinner. The dead snags became thicker, and large marks scarred the trunks.

Then rapidly the scene became grayer and grayer. There were more and stubbier snags. The scars were larger and darker. Less beauty, less vigor, less life. Uprooted trees with long dry roots like giant bony fingers clawed as if from graves. The sky grew vaster. Then, suddenly, as though falling into a dead crater, the train was in a clearing below a logged-off mountain side.

In the clearing, the snags were shorter and stouter, but sharper — daggers of pitch wood too hard to burn. Great, ugly chunks of fir with rounded, charred ends pointed up where they rested on stumps. Deep, bare, rutty skidroads, skidroad cribbing, and skidtrails[11] ran across the ground. Everything was bruised, crushed, and burnt into ugliness. There were no trees, just snags. No grass, no weeds, no birds, no life. The area of desolation extended in every direction. On the logged-over ground, the destruction was complete.

During my fifteen months of work for McDougal & Jackson, I would learn what had happened to that forest. I would learn the cause of the destruction and how it was done.

[11] *A worn path left by dragged logs.*

CHAPTER 5

A Young Man's Occupation

L UMBERJACK IS A DEROGATORY WORD with implications that any man who works as a logger — and his associates, men and women — is a rowdy bully and a person of lewd character.

The lumberjacks in the Great Lakes white pine region were homogeneous. The logging time was seasonal — from about mid-October to mid-March — and most of the lumberjacks were residents of towns near the camps. In the east, lumberjacking was in the blood. During the logging season, the crews did not move from camp to camp as they did on Puget Sound, and deep friendships developed. On Puget Sound, I do not recall meeting anyone who worked in the logging camps because they liked it. The men were always moving, there were few friends among them, and they were of many nationalities.

Puget Sound camps operated year-round. Only a few camps closed for July 4th and Christmas vacations, which each lasted a week. Except during those vacations, when a lumberjack left camp, he usually went alone and rarely met an acquaintance again. During my vacations in Seattle, Tacoma, and

Aberdeen, I met few men I knew, and they were always moochers.

A small percentage of the camp workers followed logging as an occupation. Only the experts like hooktenders, engineers, headfallers, and some rigging-men were real lumberjacks. The rest were sailors — gone broke on shore leave or trying something new — or fellows who had gone to Alaska to try their luck, railroad laborers, migrants from the east and middle west, or immigrants.

Most of the work was hard and exhausting. It was a young man's occupation. The older men were nearly always common laborers who built skidroads or did similar work.

Camp life was drab, harsh, and character-denigrating. Generally, the food was good, but the rest was depressing. The men sought escape and diversions.

Most lumberjacks worked short stretches and accumulated small stakes, which they spent on drinking — not excessively — and availing themselves of the madams on Seattle's King Street, similar streets in other cities, and lone houses near small towns like Buckley.

In contrast to the Lake Superior white pine logging camps in which alcohol was forbidden, it was not only allowed in the Puget Sound camps, it was considered proper and helpful. After a hard day's work in the cold, mud, rain, and sometimes wet snow, a good drink of whiskey was warming and invigorating. No one ever got drunk in camp, and I have no shame to admit

I was one who indulged carefully and modestly.

Besides drinking, there was also a bit of gambling — penny-ante poker and blackjack — though there was never much money with which to gamble.

The lumberjacks were a peaceful group. I never saw a fight nor any controversy that might have caused a fight. In fact, I never saw any disorder among lumberjacks, whether on the skidroads, red-light districts, or any other place.

Few of the loggers had families in the towns. I knew of only three in McDougal & Jackson's Camp 4.

With the exception of timekeeping and operating the van[12] (also known as a wonagon), no education was required to be a lumberjack. As a whole, the workers were illiterate. I wrote letters for quite a few of them.

Lumberjacks wore the same garb out of camp as in — usually calked shoes, brown tinpants during the rainy seasons and at other times, blue overalls that were often stagged below the knees. The blue flannel shirt was a general uniform. Anyone dressed better was a dude and he found the going tough. I must admit that while in the cities I was very much a man apart.

During my stay on Puget Sound, I worked in probably twenty camps. Crews consisted of from twenty to sixty men, with thirty on average.

As a whole, Puget Sound lumberjacks were hard workers and they were a good part of the population that developed

---

[12] *The camp office where supplies could be purchased.*

Puget Sound and adjacent areas into the wonderful region that it is. I am happy to have been one of those hard working and fine guys.

CHAPTER 6

Woodrats and Wool Blankets

WE ARRIVED AT CAMP 4 AFTER DINNER.[13] Carrying his turkey and blankets, Ole stepped off the train onto the slivered platform. Three loaders[14] stood waiting for mail. The woods crew had gone to work in the forest.

"Where's the bunkhouse?" Ole asked.

One of the men pointed and made an obscene wisecrack.

Ole clumsily raised his turkey and blankets to a shoulder, stepped into the mud and stumbled along the ties. Sheepishly, carrying my grip low, I followed through a gauntlet of the fellows and the train crew who glanced at each other and grinned.

"Just from the east?" asked one fellow.

I jerked my grip up in resentment.

"One of those smart Minnesota canthook experts," kidded another. "Isn't that a cute grip?"

Ole and I found our way to the bunkhouse over a creek. The flooring was so loosely fitted that I saw the water beneath and heard the rippling of the current. The roof was set on single

---

[13] *Dinner was the noon meal; supper was eaten in the evening.*
[14] *Lumberjacks responsible for loading logs onto the flatcars.*

boards. The air was chilly, and the big, round rusty stove on the sand box was cold. The board bunks, double decked along the walls, were just wide enough for one man. The whole interior was bare, and its cleaning apparently left to anyone's whim.

Bunkhouse,1917. Note the skylight and the men sitting on the deacon's seat on the left. (Courtesy of Pacific Northwest Quarterly.)

Dirty, mud-caked, discarded socks lay scattered on the floor, and stringy parts of torn blankets hung over the edge of unoccupied bunks. A few pieces of wood and chunks of bark lay in ashes on the unswept floor. Three or four improvised and overflowing sawdust-filled spittoons shoved under the bunks and deacon's seats[15] fouled the air. The seating was a few shaky

---

[15] *A bench running most of the length of a bunkhouse in a lumber camp.*

boxes and the narrow, backless, board deacon's seats that ran along the bottom of the lower bunks. Near the window at one end stood a square table where on Sundays the lumberjacks played poker and blackjack. The building was faintly lighted by a sooty skylight and two, small kerosene lamps with dirty, smoky chimneys. A few slit, torn overalls, shirts, and socks hung drying from beams. Penciled girls torn from the Police Gazette decorated an occasional bunk. Conspicuously tacked to the front wall were large pictures of prize fighters, idols like Bob Fitzsimmons and James Jeffries.

What bunk to choose? Help yourself. Anything empty, and there were a lot of empty bunks. There were no mattresses — just a little frayed straw that filtered down through cracks in the top bunks. Nice, bare, hard bunks. A bunk was a man's castle.

There were no small objects about, not even a sky pilot's[16] torn magazine. Ole cautioned me to keep anything small inside my grip — he would keep his turkey tied tight.

"Watch them damned woodrats," Ole said. "They'll haul an' carry stuff away, even y're stinky socks."

Those pesky, long-tail woodrats, sometimes called kangaroo rats by the lumberjacks, were more agile than common rats. They jumped from bunk to bunk and up and down — any place attractive to them, and it seemed all places were attractive.

---

[16] *Preachers who traveled to the camps on Sundays.*

Woodrats were intensely curious. They carried away everything, whether or not the articles were useful to them, and they hid the objects well. Many a lumberjack has been chagrined on rising to discover that his watch was gone. They moved shoes and cut the ties. If they did not move the articles, they gnawed them. The woodrats never carried things far, but they moved them to shelves, especially boxes nailed high on walls. They hopped anywhere — sometimes on lumberjacks' faces. Woodrats were stupid animals and easily trapped. But as fast as some were killed, others came in. A crew of lumberjacks never had to contend with more than three or four woodrats at one time. Those few were enough, though, and they were constant.

I saw that the blankets in the occupied bunks were a heavy wool. There were a few heavy, blue flannel shirts hanging from nails and wire clotheslines.

Ole and I selected our bunks — I took the upper one — and dumped our things on them. I shoved my new grip to the wall. I sat silently on a deacon's seat at my bunk and pushed my feet under the seat to hide my pretty shoes, even though we were alone in the bunkhouse and Ole was dopey.

Ole slumped onto the seat. With his elbows on his knees, he pressed his forehead against trembling hands. He retched.

After I had settled my things and calmed down, I stepped outside to look over the camp site and ask questions.

Camp 4 was at the end of the railroad at the base of a large valley. Ridges ran along the broad and seemingly smooth mountain sides. The area was vast. About forty miles to the southeast was snow-capped Mt. Rainier with its expansive slopes. Several tiny rivulets converged into a creek that was dammed at the camp to make a pond for floating the logs from several sections of the forest.

The camp buildings were in two rows on each side of the track that closely followed the creek. At the left were a bunkhouse, the van, the supply house, and two small shacks. A short distance further were the loading donkey[17] and the loading ramp in the pond. Along the right side, squatting on long stilts and beams over the creek, were the blacksmith shop, the cookhouse, and a bunkhouse. On the lower edge of the dam stood a large shed housing the disk grindstone, which was operated by a large paddle wheel turned by the flowing water. At the opposite end of the dam was a donkey-driven drag saw,[18] which was used to cut wood for the camp, the skidroad locomotive, and the loading donkey.

Every building was constructed of single, inch-thick, rough, fitted boards with warped battens partly covering the cracks. The roofs of the larger buildings were galvanized and corrugated iron sheeting; the smaller buildings were roofed with cedar shakes. Everything — the deacon's seats, the

---

[17] *A steam-powered winch ("donkey") identified by its function, for example, yard donkey, load donkey, and so on.*

[18] *A saw with teeth that are slanted to cut on the pulling stroke.*

benches, the tables, and the bunks — everything in the camp was made of rough, cheap lumber.

The foreman hailed me. "Where's the other fellow?"

"In the bunkhouse," I replied. "Had some spree."

The foreman and I went to the bunkhouse. Ole sat with his head resting on his arms and knees while he inhaled the steam of his vomit and urine. The foreman tapped Ole's shin with his toe and Ole slightly raised his brow, drool stringing to the floor.

"Had a tough one?" asked the foreman.

Ole drooled more as he swayed his head — unconsciously wrapping a string of the drool around his hand.

"Where's your card?" the foreman asked kindly.

I handed over my card as Ole fumbled the card out of his shirt pocket and slumped back on the deacon's seat.

The foreman examined our employment tickets.

"My name's Frank Elliot," he said. When I addressed him as "Mister," he added, "Just call me Frank."

Frank was an amiable foreman who had little to say except to question us concerning our experiences in the work we had been hired to do: bucking and working on skidroads.

I was questioned first, but not much. I was young and he could see my one qualification: I was sufficiently robust. A fellow like me could wield an ax, use a grub hoe,[19] and shovel dirt. Any bohunk[20] could do that.

---

[19] *Used to dig up roots and stumps.*
[20] *An epithet for an Eastern European laborer.*

This camp was one of the last to use horses to pull cable. A line horse carried the cable out to a log in the woods so the steam donkey could drag (skid) the log back toward it. Eventually, the steam donkeys were fitted with a haulback drum that allowed them to pull the cables themselves. (From the author's collection.)

"You'll find things different here than in Minnesota," Frank said, and he was not kidding. His face held a reassuring expression, though, and I liked him.

Frank questioned Ole quite minutely about bucking and where he had worked. Buckers had to be good at McDougal & Jackson. They must not split the logs when they sawed them into sections. Preventing the logs from splitting required patience and skill. Ole was all right. The foreman left.

Late that afternoon, Frank, Ole, and I stopped at the tool house for most of our tools, all but the bucking saw, which Ole retrieved from the sawfiler in the little shed on the dam. My tools were simple. An ax, not badly used but dull; a pointed, long-handled shovel; and a grub hoe, which was usually called a mattock. Ole's tools were a good, double-bit, long-helve ax; three broad, thin wedges in a gunnysack; a sledgehammer; and a kerosene bottle with a grooved cork and a sharp hook fastened to the neck.

I asked Ole about the bottle and he explained that because the pitch in firs was sometimes thick and abundant, the saws stuck in the cuts. They moved more easily with kerosene sprinkled on them. The hook allowed the bottle to be suspended from the side of a log. The sawfiler showed me the grindstone and how to operate it by releasing the water from the dam over the paddle wheel. No one told me how thin and sharp to grind my ax. Anyone would know that much. I had ground many axes to chop white pine, cedar, spruce, and other eastern woods. I ground my ax well and thin; that was one thing I could do. Then I honed it.

Next, I returned to the bunkhouse to show the ax to dopey Ole. He lightly slid his thumb along the edge of the blades and gauged the thickness between his thumb and forefinger.

He smiled. "Nice and thin," he said as he swung the helve to my hand. I was satisfied with my first job.

I passed the remainder of the afternoon shopping in the van and walking around the workings. I bought one double-breasted, blue wool shirt with big pearl buttons. Everybody had at least one blue wool shirt. One thick woolen blanket was all I could afford for I had left nearly all my money in the bank in Buckley. The van did not extend credit to newcomers. Knights-of-the-road sometimes disappeared. In the workings, I followed the narrow-gauge railroad bed, which was floored with planks tightly fitted between the rails. I saw lumberjacks doing many things, strange things — fallers balanced on narrow boards stuck in the trunks of trees as they chopped and sawed. I watched bucking, yarding,[21] dogging,[22] and coupling turns[23] of logs, sniping,[24] barking, and building skidroads. I watched two road donkeys pulling turns, two yard donkeys, and a swing donkey. There were two horses, one each at two widely separated places, and I watched them pull cables. I stood near big trees and at the end of butt logs higher than my head where I felt the thick, fraying bark and fingered the pitch. I inhaled so deeply, my eyes must have bulged.

[21] *The process of pulling logs from where they have been cut to a landing where they were loaded onto rail cars.*
[22] *Joining logs together end to end.*
[23] *A turn is a row of logs fastened end to end.*
[24] *Cutting one end of a log to round it, thus preventing it from gouging holes in the earth when it is dragged.*

CHAPTER 7

Hot Food and a Cold Bunk

THE AFTERNOON PASSED SLOWLY as I became increasingly restless to start work. So many kinds of jobs with so much to learn.

The air was humid and raw. The mist quickly thickened and the dusk intensified sharply. The landscape darkened quickly, and the white crown of Mt. Rainier vanished in the fog and clouds of night.

I had been sauntering in the direction of camp; now I hurried. As I approached the buildings, they appeared as dim blotches, faint yellow light filtering from the small, square windows and penciling through cracks between the boards. The slanting skylights were dull.

I felt my way to the bunkhouse and entered. Ole was sprawled in his bunk, breathing heavily. The loading crew and a few straggling lumberjacks who worked near the camp arrived first. The men worked until nightfall at that time of the year, and they continued to do so until the days were long enough for them to work twelve hours in daylight. The men who worked at a distance left the camp before daylight and returned after dusk. Everything to do with handling big timber had to be done in full light. Steam-power logging in big timber was dangerous work. Much more dangerous than in the east.

The intensifying chill of the misty Puget Sound air was paining. The part-time bullcook[25] built a fire in the large stove made from an iron oil barrel. The stinky bunkhouse warmed except along the shaky walls. The little lights were so dim that men's faces were indistinguishable. I went to my bunk and sat on the deacon's seat.

The men came in, first singly, then in pairs or little groups, and finally a large group that I recognized by their talk as belonging to the skidroad crew. All except the crew foreman were foreigners, mostly Scandinavians and Southern Europeans, each of whom spoke his own language and jargon. All the true lumberjacks wore blue wool shirts and tinpants, all had calked shoes. The foreigners wore long, pointed shoes, queer jackets, and flat-brimmed hats. Just arrived from across the ocean. Two or three had rubber sailor hats.

Tinpants, also known as paraffinpants, were so called because they were stiff. They were made of brown duck that was re-enforced with some sort of stuff said to be paraffin that rendered them waterproof. When first purchased, the pants were folded flat and looked like brown tin. For a few days while they were being broken in, they chafed badly, but they soon took the shape of the owner's legs and could stand in a corner without

---

[25] *One who does caretaking jobs in a logging camp, especially helping the cook.*

collapsing. One had to be careful not to put them near heat. When a man stepped into them, it was like pushing his legs in to two lengths of iron stovepipe.

Quickly the men dispersed. There was no chumming and no conversation. Some hurried to change from calked shoes and tinpants to lighter shoes and ordinary overalls stagged above their shoe tops. A few superficially washed with cold water in rusty basins on a bench outside the door, then threw the dirty water behind themselves in the track, where it became slimy, or over the platform into the creek. Each man had his own towel — if he had one at all — that was stiff with dirt. Those who lacked towels used their shirt sleeves or the edge of their blankets. Each man purchased his own soap, but few had it. Every item for comfort and sanitation was a lumberjack's affair — employers furnished only the straw for the bunks. I heard that a few logging camps had mattresses, and later I did run into such a camp on the Tacoma & Eastern Railroad. Those mattresses were full of bedbugs, fleas, and lice.

Casually, someone ventured a short remark about an experience during the day, but that was not addressed to anyone in particular. A woodrat jumped out of a piled blanket. It brought a shower of shoes, and the pest escaped amid oaths. The dusty, small lamps dangled palely from wires. The air along the wall was chilly and damp. The stove soon radiated intense heat. A man was uncomfortable whether near or far from the stove. On one side the chill pressed against the skin, while on the other side the fire burned. Burned in front and chilled behind, he kept on turning like barbecue.

Only inadvertently did anyone notice anyone else, not even newcomers, not even somebody from the east nor a foreigner with odd clothes and shoes. Newcomers came too often to be noticed before supper. There were no acquaintances to greet. Puget Sound logging was a shuffling industry of the worst kind.

I was an ambitious kid — nineteen and too sensitive — in an environment much different from what I had expected and in which I was to find it difficult to adjust myself. It was an environment permeated with an atmosphere of coolness, almost total indifference, uncouth, and excessively rough. While waiting for supper, some of the fellows began to make remarks about going to town, and they elaborated on what they would do there. And their talk was about — well, they were single, unattached, and they were lumberjacks, sailors, and other laborers.

Clang, clang, clang! The dinner gong — a piece of iron rail struck with a heavy iron rod — sounded. Up jumped the hungry men. They rushed through the door. I stepped to the door as the gang bolted by. Down the track they strode, hopped, or just walked slowly as they sought firm footing, sinking calks in the ties and splashing in the mud puddles. No running, just aggressive going. I could see their forms against the cookhouse light, cursing the Oregon mist.

I returned to Ole. "Come on, fellow, supper."

Ole pushed himself out of his bunk and walked uncertainly at my side. Mouth goo had gray-streaked Ole's hands. He did not wash.

I saw the shadowy, swaying forms enter the cookhouse door. Glistening raindrops streaked against the light.

"Just from the east?" asked a big man at my side when I hesitated at the door. His voice was friendly.

"Minnesota, Northern Minnesota," I replied. "Hired out in Seattle." I liked that man right away.

As he stepped into the cookhouse, he hooked the tobacco cud from his mouth, and I noticed his stubby, fingerless right hand.

"How're the gals down by the bridge, Abe?" somebody asked.

After stamping the mud from our shoes, we entered the cookhouse and stopped at a stove to rewarm ourselves.

"I come from Minnesota, too," he said. "Long ago. That's when the timber was big there. I hear it's gone now."

"Almost," I said.

"Ever hear of Paul Bunyan and Babe his pet ox? Any blue snow lately?" The lumberjack massaged the stub of his hand. I glanced at my own dirty hands as I rubbed them together.

"Come on Rutherford," jibed a voice. "Stop kidding the kid."

But Abe Rutherford, the headfaller, was not kidding. A

lasting friendship was made then.

The workers swung to the right or to the left, making bee-lines for their places — just like in the eastern logging camps. There were a few things alike after all. Ole and I were the last to be ready for supper. We stood at one side as the last man took his place at a table. After they had all been seated, the cookee waved us to separate places at the long, oilcloth-covered tables.

Poking one foot and then the other over the bench, I squeezed between two fellows. One was muddy and wet — the other's tinpants were pitch shiny.

Tin plates clanged as they were slammed in front of us. Hands grabbed forks and speared the choicest food, grabbing pie and other desserts first, needlessly fearing that there would not be enough to go around. Those men were hungry, and manners were primitive. No talking, just "Pass this" or "Pass that." General conversation was forbidden. They ate and gulped, and they ate much. When they were through, they left. No loitering. They ate inside and talked outside.

The cookhouse interior was like that of the bunkhouse, rough lumber everywhere, but it was clean. All the dishes — plates, cups, bowls, and round platters were tin, and some of the larger containers were made of tin cans. Black iron knives, forks, and spoons completed the equipment. The fellows conveyed food into their mouths with their knives, then jabbed the knives into the bowls of butter.

McDougal & Jackson fed their men well. The over-all bill

of fare throughout my employment there included fresh and salt meats of all kinds and fresh salmon and halibut. Sundays we had little clams and Olympia oysters — those good little oysters. Later I learned that some of the camps provided dog salmon,[26] which was bony and sometimes stinky. There were nice apples in boxes near the door. Help yourself. Had to have apples in Washington. Canned fruits. Lots of canned fruits, and plenty of fresh vegetables from Puyallup Valley, and fresh milk from those acre ranches around Buckley.

The piercing calks slivered the floor. The rain spattered on the roof, and sprayed in. Some of the men sneaked cookies into their pockets as the cookee looked away.

By bedtime — nine o'clock — I had become quite aware of the penetrating chill that caused constant discomfort. As the lumberjacks rolled into their bunks and pulled heavy blankets tightly around themselves, it was apparent that the blanket that I had bought in the van and my flimsy clothing could not keep me warm. Nearly everybody went to bed in their heavy clothes, including socks. If a lumberjack was wet he changed — if he had dry clothes. If not, he slept in what he had on and steamed until he dried. Those lumberjacks slept under primitive conditions, except that they were not lousy. Each had his private blankets so that there was little personal contact — a condition unavoidable in eastern logging camps.

---

[26] *Chum salmon (Oncorhynchus keta), a species of anadromous fish in the salmon family.*

Those lumberjacks were grimy. Continuous washing with cold water, usually without soap, constant working in mud, contact with oil and ashes from the donkeys and locomotives, and fluid pitch from the logs made their skin gray and harsh. Some fellows scattered the frayed straw and arranged their blankets in an orderly way, spreading one blanket over the straw and the other over themselves. They did not have quilts, which were too bulky to pack and carry about and did not dry readily. Anyway, quilts were for ladies and dudes. A pillow was anything that made a hump. Turkeys and shoes made fine pillows.

The fire in the big stove burned out. At nine o'clock, the bullcook put out the lights. Ole was snoring. I climbed to the upper bunk and snuggled under that blanket. After trying to get comfortable, I was on the bare boards. Somebody shifted and cursed the cold. Heavy breathing, a cough. Thump, thump — a woodrat was hopping about. Something was dragged across the floor. A low oath. Another oath, but much louder. Silence again — just the rain. The cold was agonizing, the boards grew harder, and my underside began to pain. I had overlooked the fact that air is enveloping, that blankets on top did not shut off cold from below. I tucked the edges of my blanket under myself. The cold progressively pricked. The rain unceasingly spattered on the roof, and some sprayed on my head. Oh that Oregon mist in March! Ole groaned.

I had been reminded of my recent arrival from the east,

and now I was perfectly aware of being in a logging camp on the side of a mountain in the Puget Sound country.

"Wait until you get to Grays Harbor," Abe had said. "You ain't seen nothin' yet."

Morning. The bullcook lit the little oil lamps and called, "Roll out!" The woodrats scurried. Shoes thumped on the floor and the calks crunched the boards, all except my shoes and those of the foreigners. The tin wash pans clanged as cold water was splashed into the creek and onto the track. Slime and stink, wiping with dirty towels, shirt sleeves, anything, or just rubbing bare hands.

Through the diffused, dull light in the open door, I saw patches of white. Snow. Rain and snow were falling. Cold, seeping slush. Lumberjacks cursed the rain and snow. A fellow shivered going to work, steamed all day, and then shivered at night.

The calling gong clanged. Down the track we went, calks crunching on the ties. My rubbers splashed through the cindery mud and slid.

The cookhouse was well lit and warm. The air was fragrant with the scent of good food. The rush of the lumberjacks, and the clang of dishes. Good, steaming coffee in the big tin pots, milk in cans, bacon, eggs, and pancakes with thick syrup. Crisp pancakes right from the top of the big stove, and sticky steamed pancakes that the lumberjacks avoided. The cookee hurried between the tables and to the stove and back again along the tables. He was like a guard. Breakfast was hot and good and nourishing in the McDougal & Jackson camp.

CHAPTER 8

About Skidroads

T HE MORNING WAS STILL DARK as we scattered out of the cookhouse. At the edge of the pond, the loading donkey blew steam, and fine sparks flitted from the smokestack. The fireman had woken early to light the fuel.

After breakfast, while the men waited for the locomotive whistle to call them out, they sat by their bunks or stuffed things into their turkeys to hide them from the woodrats. I sat on the deacon's seat apprehensive of the jibes about my rubbers and that I was from the east. One man at the other end of the bunkhouse sarcastically remarked to the head loader, "Ground man for you, Bill. Don't let him break all the canthooks."

The first afternoon, when I had observed the camp's activities, I had watched the loading crew pile forty-foot logs onto the flatcars. There were no canthooks in sight, for a canthook would have been as useful to load those big logs as a lever would have been to tilt Mt. Rainier.

An aging man nibbling at his Spearhead plug sat at my side with his elbows on his knees. He pulled his leather gloves smoothly through his hands.

"Going to work on the skidroad or swamp?" he asked.

"Skidroad," I replied in a low voice.

"Don't let him dig too deep," called a lumberjack across the room.

"Ah, shut up. He'll be a hooktender before you know it," came a rebuke.

"Don't let him climb too high," said another fellow as he glanced at my rubbers.

More glances at my rubbers crammed under the deacon's seat. Snappily I swung my feet out and planted them firmly for anyone to see. Straw and chaff stuck in my clothes and itched.

"Boy, d'I sleep," Ole said with a yawn, red eyes blinking. "How about you, Bill?" he said, addressing me. That started a new nickname for me, and it stuck.

I made no reply, just grinned and nodded. I was determined to say little. I would just show them.

The skidroad locomotive's whistle blew and the crew filed out. Old Oregon had sent another miserable mist.

"Come with me," the foreman said to me in a kindly voice and a motion of his head.

"New man for you, Fred," he said. "Don't let him break too many canthooks." He patted my arm in friendly gesture.

Fred was the skidroad boss. In a few days he would be Uncle Fred St. Clair to me.

Passing the sawfiler's shed at the edge of the dam, I saw the fallers and buckers selecting their glistening saws that were racked upright along the walls. The forms of the two yard-line horses were distinguishable as they went up the narrow-gauge railroad to the sides, each side being an area where one yarding crew logged.

Calked shoes crunched along the planks and ties. Someone slipped on a rail and cursed.

Uncle Fred, with me at his heels, turned right into the skidroad. Some singsong by the Swedes, harsh guttural Ks from the Finns, and indistinguishable sounds from others. An Italian beautifully hummed, "O Solo Mio."

"What's your name?" asked Uncle Fred. I told him my first name. "Your last name," he insisted. I told him.

"French Canadian," he remarked, pleased.

"Yes, but born in Michigan," I said. "Up in Paul Bunyan's country."

"Me, too. I'm Canadian. Born by Quebec. Spoke nothin' but French when I come to this country by Sault Ste. Marie forty years ago. But I forget it all. Ain't that funny?"

"I speak and read French now," I said. "I'm a pretty good frog."

Uncle Fred tried to frame some French sentences, but he uttered only disconnected words.

As the morning lightened, we walked more briskly. Uncle Fred chatted and nibbled his plug. We passed the end of an abandoned skidroad. Big drops of icy water fell from the branches and plunked on our skins.

"Built that one. Built the skidroads for McDougal & Jackson for a long time," Uncle Fred remarked proudly as he tugged at his scraggly mustache.

Forms were becoming more distinct in the mist, and I was fascinated.

Our conversation lagged a bit, then Uncle Fred said, "We'll go to Seattle together July 4th. Have a hell of a good time. You stay with me. Ever go on King Street?"

We walked faster. We passed some fallers and buckers who were inspecting and arranging their tools. They could not fell or buck before full daylight, because they had to take the bearings of the trees. Passing, I heard an oath, an obscene joke.

The mist was rising, the gray light clearing. The rails appeared gray and yellow, rusty from the damp. Objects took form. There were tall stumps with notches in their sides, snags, broken trunks, crushed treetops, and tangled branches. Long, deep, rough furrows like ditches ran along the ground. I saw bruised stumps, then large, deep-brown, splintered fir logs with crushed green trees among them. There were large spruce, cedar, and hemlock, their branches torn and trunks stripped by the firs that had smashed through them. There were spiky-looking trees and pitchy butts and short stumps. Then, smack in front of us was the grand forest, the forest that would soon be ravaged.

The narrow skid railroad ended at the edge of the trees that were waiting to be slaughtered. There we entered onto a

Pulling a turn of logs on a cross-skid skidroad near Vancouver, Canada.

new skidroad that had been completed for some distance. The timber had not been cut except in the narrow corridor. The corridor was about twenty feet wide and, with the tall forest on each side, resembled a great canyon.

Skidroads were of two types of construction: the cross-skid and the fore-an-aft. Sometimes a skidroad had parts of both. By the spring of 1907, the cross-skid was obsolete. They had been used when oxen or horses rather than steam donkeys pulled the logs. The older men who had experienced oxen and horse logging said the cross-skids were much better when animal power was all that was available, and that grease was sometimes put on the skids to make the logs slide along more easily.

Fore-an-aft skidroad with a steam donkey.

The fore-an-aft skidroad was constructed with tree trunks of any length that were laid lengthwise, so that turns slid along the grain. Although there was much more friction between the logs and the fore-an-afts than with the cross-skids, the fore-an-afts were not so easily displaced and, thus, more durable. Cross-skids had to be laid in firm ground, but fore-an-afts could be laid in any ground regardless of the terrain. Long fore-an-afts spanned creeks and small gullies, and sometimes they were laid on cribbing that was quite high.

The skidroad crew was made up of three separate sets of men, each with its own boss and each having a distinct task to perform. Sometimes the three crews overlapped.

To advance up the skidroad, the two fallers, who were

also the swampers,[27] were in the lead; next came the donkey crew made up of the hooktender,[28] a rigging-slinger,[29] a signalman[30] (or signalpunk), the fireman, and the engineer; last were the common laborers who cut the fallen trunks into skids, dug the trenches to lay them in, then leveled the ground.

Old Anton Benson was the swamper for the skidroad. Anton had been with McDougal & Jackson for several years, and he had always done the same work. He was well along in years when we became acquainted. I respected his ability, and we became close friends.

Anton was of Swedish ancestry, though he had come to America when he was quite young. He still spoke Swedish and he retained that peculiar, and very pleasant, singsong accent. Anton liked to crack jokes about Swedes. "Ya, Anton, he ban a damned fine roundhead," he would say of himself. After I became skidroad hooktender, Anton and I had many consultations with Uncle Fred St. Clair, the skidroad foreman, with whom we had to coordinate our work. French Canadian jargon, Swedish singsong. I greatly enjoyed it.

There usually were about fifteen laborers in the crew.

---

[27] *Men who cleared brush and trimmed branches from logs. Wilfred said this was not a Puget Sound term, but these jobs had no title, so he applied "swamper" to them. The term has its origins circa 1857 in the southern United States to refer to a workman who cleared roads for a timber faller in a swamp.*

[28] *Boss of the yarding crew.*

[29] *The hooktender's helper.*

[30] *Provided communication between a crew working in the timber or along a skidroad and the donkey engineer when he was too far away to hear.*

Each morning, they resumed the jobs where they had left off the night before. The men used long-handled and round-ended shovels, mattocks, or dull axes to cut roots as they dug. Two or three cleared away the debris ahead, and an inexperienced sawyer bucked the felled trees into eight-foot skids. Others took peaveys[31] to turn the skids and place them crossways to the direction of the road if they were building a cross-skidroad. This was the only job I saw peaveys used for in the western forests.

The fog cleared early but returned to pour again as Oregon mist. My clothes were soon soaked and heavy with clay. They stuck to my skin and the water seeped through my felt hat — that nice hat from the east. Some of the bohunks had fishermen's rubber hats; others worked bareheaded. I blew water from the tip of my nose all day. Everything was slick under my rubbers — the bark on the logs and the putty clay. Those rubbers just sloshed about, and my toes squished in the water, which fell on my head and slid along my body. I cut holes in my rubbers like the other men cut holes in their shoes, so the water squirted out and the mud oozed in. Everyone was soaked. I was soaked and cold.

Uncle Fred showed me how to dig in the clay to create a good trench for a skid, how to cut the roots and smash the rocks with the sledgehammer. The trench had to be just right. When I thought my trench was ready, Uncle Fred measured both the trench and the skid with my shovel handle.

---

[31] *Peaveys are similar to canthooks but have pointed metal ends.*

"All right," said Uncle Fred, using a peavey to give the skid a roll and flop it into place. It fit. Uncle Fred's mouth activated like a little bellows. "Das good job," he said.

We ate dinner at the site. The bullcook brought the food on the locomotive. Though it was just as good as it had been in the cookhouse, the Oregon mist and the hairy moss from the branches mixed with it, and I was reminded of food freezing on our plate's in the logging camps of Northern Minnesota and Michigan, except here the food was soaked. But my, that hot coffee was good.

After dinner, Uncle Fred assigned me to knot skids that had been cut from hemlocks and felled trees. Jauntily, I picked up my sharp ax, felt the blades and swung it several times to show off. This, thought I, was something that I could do with the rest of them. I could chop. I had chopped lots of soft white pine. However, my first experience with Puget Sound hemlock was quite educational relative to the quality of different woods. Puget Sound hemlocks were beautiful, and they had few knots except at the tops. They did not grow nearly as large around as firs nor as tall; however, the trunks were as straight and uniform. I had been told that they made the best abrasion skids because the wood was harder than fir and it resisted better. On the cleared ground just ahead of the skids there were trunks of hemlock trimmed and cut into proper lengths. The skids averaged about two feet in diameter at the small end and a number of them were cut from each tree.

Sled for a steam donkey, circa 1922. The sled pulled itself using a cable attached to a tree or other solid anchor.

I was delighted with my assignment because it was clean work. Although my rubbers slipped when I stood on the bark to chop, the ground where the skids lay was not muddy; the trenches, unfinished the night before, were partly filled with water.

I swung my ax with vim. I started by chopping the butt off the splintered part at the undercut. Then I walked along the trunk, knocking off dry spikes and fine branches. My sharp ax cut smoothly as the little branches dropped. The branches became larger and larger as I proceeded; they were tougher and more brittle, and the cutting required heavier strokes. Then it took two blows, one on each side of the branch, or one under and one on top, and not too near the trunk. The best way was to cut the branches and then trim the knots. Finally, I reached the large branches. They had to be chopped off, not just clipped. The wood was much harder. The zing of the ax became louder, and the zing was loudest when I was trimming the knot crossway to the grain. The knots were brittle. They broke into little pieces that hit my face. The ax was sinking into the wood with difficulty and each knot required many blows.

Knotting of the hemlock was slow. I grew impatient. I swung my ax at arm's length at the base of a limb. I heard a dull snap, and as I swung my ax back for another blow, I saw something shining in the jagged cut. The object was different from the greenish bark and the blueish wood and it was about an inch long and thin. I stopped and felt the thing. It was made of steel. I raised my ax to examine the bit. There was a deep, inchlong crescent nick in one bit. I extracted the piece of bit from the wood and looked around, feeling foolish. With a single stroke, I had learned that hemlock knots were the hardest wood I had chopped. No wonder lumberjacks hated hemlock.

Building a skidroad was like pressing a gigantic dagger into the vitals of the forest.

The foreman of the camp figured the course of the road and marked it by blazing the trees. We could not deviate from the course. The swampers at the head of the advancing skidroad cut the brush and carried it to one side. They felled the smaller trees, leaving high stumps, which could be more easily pulled out by the donkey. The trees of the desired size for skids were bucked where they fell. The trees less than a foot thick remained standing until the donkey arrived to pull them over. The stumps that were too large to be pulled by the donkey were blasted with dynamite.

The donkey crew that followed the swampers had a small, old-fashioned donkey yarder. The donkey sled was longer, but narrower than the sleds of the larger donkeys, and we took unusual chances when we moved it on rough ground.

The cable used for clearing a skidroad was always an old one and broke frequently, which necessitated splicing each time. Every hooktender was an expert cable splicer, a task that he disliked because the worn wire broke, piercing his gloves and lacerating his hands.

A good skidroad over which to pull Puget Sound timber was as superior to a Michigan skidroad as the Union Pacific Railroad was superior to the Oregon Trail. Pulling turns of six to ten logs that were twenty-four to forty-feet long each as far as a mile using one-and-one-eighth-inch steel cables with a powerful steam donkey was a whole lot different than skidding twelve- to sixteen-foot white pine logs with a team of horses.

Although not laid out, planned, or designed by engineers trained in mathematical computation and in the use of instruments, the skidroad was the result of ingenuity and skill. The only instrument used was the camp foreman's compass. There were no notes, no maps, no blueprints — just section and quarter-section corner marks and blazed trees on the lines.

The camp foremen were the surveyors. The skidroad bosses and the skidroad hooktenders were the construction engineers. They directed grading of the roadbed and the laying of the cross-skids and fore-an-afts. They erected bridges and cribbings with timber, and they fitted them together to withstand the pounding, jarring, and wear by the logs.

CHAPTER 9

Puget Sound Timber

FOUR KINDS OF TIMBER WERE LOGGED on Puget Sound in 1906: Douglas fir (commonly called yellow fir), cedar, spruce, and hemlock. Their values varied according to the transportation facilities available, the size and equipment at sawmills, and market demand. Each of these timbers is different from those of the same names in other parts of the United States.

DOUGLAS FIR is the most important tree growing in the great forests of Puget Sound and Grays Harbor. Tall and unusually symmetrical, a single trunk could yield as many as five forty-foot, knot-free logs. Douglas fir is not as churn-butted[32] and flute-butted[33] as cedar. The roots begin to spread near the ground, and the trunk tapers more gradually. The branches are comparatively short and slender for such large trees, and they are bunched at the top. The thick, deeply grooved bark is rich brown. When the bark is dry, it is more crumbly than the bark of other trees and

---

[32] *A churn-butt is an expansion of the lower end of the tree trunk above the usual stump flare found in all species.*
[33] *Flutes are folds in the surface, extending upward from the base of the tree.*

burns so readily that even when the trees are green, a forest fire is difficult to bring under control.

Firs averaging from five to six feet in diameter are common; larger ones are scarce. The largest I saw scaled ten feet in diameter inside the bark, which was about six inches thick.

The wood of the Douglas fir is light yellow, and when the wood is skillfully milled, the grain is beautiful. The best wood is used for flooring.

Red fir, more common in Oregon, is not so large nor tall as the Douglas fir; however, the trees are quite similar. The bark of the red fir is somewhat redder and smoother. The wood is also redder and its quality inferior because it is more brittle and splits more easily. Red fir is more likely to be cut into timber and railroad ties.

Douglas fir resists decay well. Many large trees have been windfalls[34] for centuries, and, with the exception of the sap, the wood of a windfall is as sound as that of standing trees.

CEDAR trunks are fully used, because even the chunks, if they are longer than a shingle, can be cut into shingle bolts.[35] The properties of the cedar are quite different from those of other trees. Except in the stump, the grain is long and straight, and the fiber is soft and resilient. It is more resistant to decay. The wood splits easily so that in the days before shingles were readily available, much of it was split into shakes and used for

---

[34] *A tree, usually old and dead, blown to the ground by the wind.*
[35] *A block of wood from which shingles will be cut.*

roofing and siding. After lumber mills were built, cedar was almost entirely made into shingles. The men who worked in the shingle mills were called shingle-weavers.

Puget Sound cedar is tall, and when it grows with other trees in thick stands, the thin branches are well up to the top. The butt is usually hollow and in sections.

After the cedar in the rich-soil valleys was removed and the land was being cleared for the tiny ranches, the tall stumps were cut into shingle bolts and shipped to the mills. The money received for the sale of those bolts provided a substantial income for the rancher.

SPRUCE grows almost entirely in swamps along the streams and in the lowlands along the coast. At one time, Grays Harbor was famous for its particularly large and clear spruce. The upland spruce is smaller, and the trunks are not so clear of knots nor of as high quality.

Spruce trees grow scattered among the firs and can be logged at the same time and with the same equipment. Spruce also float well.

The branches are long and wavy and, near the trunk, large, tough, and hard. Sometimes, when a spruce falls, the large stubs of broken branches are driven into the ground. To fell such spruce requires chopping those stubs, a job more difficult than chopping trees of the same size. The grain of the wood at the butt is unusually curly and tough. During early logging days, fallers cut the stumps several feet high to avoid the tough butt wood and to decrease the size of what they had to cut.

Before 1910, nearly all the Puget Sound and Grays Harbor spruce were sliced into veneer to make crates and baskets for berries, apples, peaches, and vegetables. For several years after the invention of the airplane, the best spruce went into the construction of airplane wings and gliders. During World War I, the United States government, under Army supervision, operated many spruce camps.

HEMLOCK was the least desirable of the four timbers, although there were many more of them than of cedar and spruce. The trees were smaller with fewer logs in a trunk. Until recently,[36] only the smooth portion of the hemlock trunk had value; the knots were so hard that lumberjacks avoided them. In many camps, hemlock were used for skids or left to burn.

During the years that logs were driven in streams, hemlock logs were left behind. They were so heavy, especially at the butt, that, in shallow water, they would have sunk[37] and obstructed other logs. The finished lumber of the hemlock has a faint blue tint, and the grain is distinctly flat. The wood is more brittle and harder than that of fir. The depletion of fir greatly increased the value and usefulness of hemlock, and by 1910 hemlock was being logged along with the other timbers if transportation was available.

---

[36] *"Recently" would have been in the 1950s.*
[37] *Thus, they were called "sinkers."*

CHAPTER 10

Death of a Giant

FAR ENOUGH BEHIND THE SKIDROAD CREW for their safety, the fallers felled the timber. The heavy trees could not be permitted to fall across the skidroad because their crushing impact displaced the skids.

Fallers had the greatest responsibility of any lumberjacks working in big timber. The degree of their skill accounted for certain factors that they alone could control, such as the difference between sawing or destroying the falling trees, and crushing or preserving the small trees, and whether the yarding was easy or difficult. Thousands of feet of fine timber in a single tree were sometimes destroyed because of a small difference in pay between good and bad fallers.

The branches of a large fir did not protect the fir as it fell through other trees and landed. If a fir fell across a stump, windfall or logs, it smashed and splintered for many feet on each side of the point of impact. Because the middle logs were the best, and usually the ones broken, the damage could be particularly extensive. The top log was knotty and of low grade, and the butt was usually pitch-seamed and suitable only for coarse lumber. Yet because timber was so plentiful on Puget Sound, it was not profitable to clean an area to avoid breakage.

Fallers on their springboards. (From the author's collection.)

McDougal & Jackson employed only the best fallers. They were closely supervised and commanded to take ample time and care in their work. No attention was given to the protection and preservation of small trees or large, unwanted timber — especially the hemlock.

Fallers worked in pairs — the headfaller and secondfaller. The former usually received twenty-five cents more per day than the latter. Their tools were a seven-foot, slender crosscut saw (one or two longer crosscut saws were available for larger trees); two long and thin narrow-bit axes with long slender helves; three or four broad, long, thin, metal wedges; a sledgehammer; two oil bottles with a hook on each for fastening to the bark; an eight-foot measuring-stick; and two springboards on which to stand while they were felling.

Felling a single tree might require a half-day or more, and despite a lack of systematic, scientific, and engineering skills, the job could be astonishingly well done.

Let us go back to 1906 to see the skillful felling of a large Douglas fir in Camp 4.

There stands the three-hundred-foot giant, among other firs, hemlocks, an occasional cedar, and one spruce. A rich-brown Douglas fir, symmetrical and seemingly straight. Surrounding its base are ferns and small bushes. Green moss clings to its exposed roots. It is a thing of strength, firmness, and great weight. In defiance of the winds and storms from the Pacific Ocean, it has grown for centuries. After it falls, there will be a void in the green canopy that will remain forever.

The headfaller walks to the fir, looking up as he approaches. He is Abe Rutherford, one of the best fallers on Puget

Sound. Abe Rutherford with the stubby right hand.

He ascends the roots, places his hand against the trunk and sights up along the sides. To the inexperienced eye, the tree appears erect, horizontal to the plane of the earth. However, trees are never perfectly erect. They lean slightly, and the trunks are always curved.

Ahead of Abe are the trees of the vast forest, and behind him are stumps, windfalls, logs, stripped hemlocks, cedars, spruce, and tangles of brush and boughs. The big tree must fall ahead into the forest and lie prostrate throughout its entire length unless the lean of the fir is such that Abe cannot prevent it from falling backward or sideways or on uneven ground.

Abe takes his ax and holds the loose end of the helve between the thumb and forefinger of his left hand. The ax hangs like a plumb. He sights up the helve like a hunter sights his rifle. He walks around the fir and stops and plumbs. Finally, he points out to the secondfaller the direction in which the fir will fall.

In its downward plunge, a large fir may turn as it strikes other trees. Its momentum is not slackened by them, and it crushes everything under it. It breaks if the bed is not level, and the bucker must make extra cuts to cull the splintered parts, which become a hindrance to yarding and can provide fuel for forest fires.

Finally, Abe looks up along the trunk and examines the branches for broken stubs and loose hanging limbs — known as widowmakers. If he sees any, he can either take the risk of felling the tree or wait until another fir smashes into this one and strips its limbs. He sees no widowmakers.

The secondfaller has brought the tools and placed them at the base of the fir. Each faller has his long, narrow-bit ax and oil bottle. One will chop left handed and one right handed.

The fallers climb the tree's churn-butt. They each notch the tree in three places so there are two notches near the front of the trunk, two in the middle on opposite sides from each other, and two near the back. They insert the calk ends of their springboards into the front notches. They rest the long, slender felling-saw upright against the fir and hang the kerosene bottles in the bark. Each faller jumps up and hooks his chest over his springboard, then slowly raises himself and stands. They are now ready to fell the giant. In a few hours what has required centuries to grow will be prostrate.

With their axes, the fallers slice away the thick bark to keep the needle-sharp points of the saw's teeth from growing dull on the sand and grit the wind has pounded into the bark.

The headfaller grabs one handle of the saw and swings the other handle to the secondfaller. Then each takes his oil bottle and sprinkles both sides of the saw so it will slide easily.

The fallers adjust the teeth of the saw against the wood, then draw it back and forth slowly. They continue that procedure until the saw is fully sunk into the wood. When they have cut to the required depth for the undercut, the back of the cut is evened into a straight line.

Then, with axes, they define the angled cut they will make in the tree. Rhythmically, they alternately swing their axes — grunting and whiffing at each stroke. Then they start over again, four inches higher. They repeat this procedure until the rough undercut is made.

The fallers jump down, unhook their boards, then insert them into the back notches. This is where they will stand to saw down that big tree. The secondfaller places the sack with the wedges just below the springboard. The fallers climb up onto the boards.

They take up the saw and oil it, then start the saw in the same manner that they did for the undercut, only it is two inches higher than the bottom of the undercut, which will help to control the tree's fall. The saw zips into the wood, at first in short strokes, then longer, then the men go into full swing the lengths of their arms. Yellow sawdust with a pitchy aroma swishes out of each side and drops in graceful curves.

The fir is so erect that it pinches the saw. With his ax Abe chips the wood from the back of the cut. He jumps to the ground and dumps the wedges out of the sack. He inserts the wedges into the cut and taps them with his sledgehammer until they stick in place. Together they saw the corner to the required depth, then, after re-adjusting their springboards, they saw the other corner. Finally, they saw across the back.

The cut is opened slightly, releasing the saw. The pitch

flies out of the cut and splatters the fallers' tinpants. The sawing continues until each end of the undercut is sawed.

The right amount of unsawed wood must be left to hold the fir and control the direction of its fall.

The headfaller jumps off his springboard. Fine moss and debris float down from the branches. He compares the uncut corners with the depth of the cut and the lean of the tree. There is no hurry in felling this fir because it is particularly valuable.

Abe climbs up on his board and the two men pound the wedges — first one and then the other. At each blow, the top of the fir quivers. Dust and needles, cones and bits of twigs fall thicker and thicker. Both men look again for widowmakers. Then they saw again, half circling the tree. They pound the wedges hard, and as they pound and saw — a bit on one side, then the other side and then across the back — the wood begins to crack and pull apart just back of the undercut. The cut opens slowly and then faster. The wood cracks and pulls and cracks. But the fir does not waver and the wood breaks at the undercut.

The fallers jump from their springboards and insert them into the front notches. Each chops a large notch a foot or more deep and as wide in the undercut. The notch will prevent the tree from splitting.

The fallers continue to saw and pound the wedges. The cut opens and the wood cracks louder and they feel the slivers hold the saw's teeth. The air under the branches grows dustier — more dirt, fir needles, twigs. They watch for widowmakers.

Sidetrack and part of the crew of Camp 4, along with wives and children from town. (From the author's collection.)

Then the wedges loosen and the saw wiggles and trembles. The fallers throw the wedges and the sledgehammer out of the way. They glance up the trunk while they saw furiously — they must cut all the wood that they can before they scurry away.

The cut opens and the top of the fir shifts, and as it does the crown shivers and wavers like a beaten giant in his last defiance.

"Timber –er –er –er," loudly and ominously shout the fallers. This is no joke — that tree is tall and will descend a long way. The broken branches, the fir's knots, other firs, hemlocks, and other trees will be hurled far by the powerful tree as it smashes among them. They will bend like great springs, then release. The burst of air as the great top falls will be cyclonic.

The fallers' strokes grow long and jerky. The saw's teeth hook more and more in the slivers as the wood pulls apart. The crown of the falling fir gains momentum in its downward plunge.

"Timber –er –er –er!"

CRACK! The wood at the stump breaks. Wedges plump to the ground or lie flat on the stump. Sawing stops.

"Let 'er go!" Abe commands. The fallers jerk their spring-boards from the stump and dash to shelter behind a big tree.

"Timber! Timber –er –er –er! Timber –er –er, –er!"

The crown of the fir quivers more violently as the air swirls. The branches and the trunk strip the smaller trees, which bend and rebound, throwing loose branches all about. The wood at the stump is broken: the fir is loose. Its great body crashes and bucks against the ground — a giant's dying agony. The crown with all its branches is crushed. As it plunges through the air, the area is covered with loose leaves, twigs, needles, moss, and branches where they will be left to dry and burn, destroying everything that remains.

The fallers return to the stump and gather their tools. Falling a giant, pitchy-seamed fir is grueling and exhausting work. But the headfaller does not rest long.

Abe takes his ax and measuring stick and struggles through the broken branches to the crown of the tree. As he walks along that trunk, he examines the ground as well as stumps and trees along the trunk's side. He looks for conks and breaks, for it is he who must judge where the bucker will buck the tree and make the best logs.

Logs at the tree butt that are quite pitch-seamed are cut twenty-four feet long — the shortest length allowed. Second and third logs — the best — are cut forty feet long. The other logs are cut somewhere between those two lengths.

Abe examines the end of the butt for pitch seams. If there are few and they are thin and do not extend far up, he will measure the butt log as long as possible. But if the seams are thick and wide and the wood of low quality, he will measure the butt log to twenty-four feet.

Abe must also take into consideration the angle at which the logs lay to the skidroad. If the top of the fir points toward the skidroad he will measure all the logs as long as possible. The butt log is always harder to yard if its large end has to be pulled forward.

In this fir, Abe measures one twenty-four-foot butt log, two forty-foot logs, a thirty-two-foot log, and a twenty-eight-foot log.

Another giant is dead.

CHAPTER 11

From Stump to Flatbed

WINTER LOGGING IN THE GREAT LAKES REGION was so similar in all camps that the description of the operations in one camp was sufficient to describe, in a general way, the work and equipment in all other camps. But a general description was not applicable to Puget Sound logging.

Some plans and operations were standard, such as yarding, skidroad-hauling, and loading, but a camp also might have features differing greatly from other camps. Methods were in constant evolution and experimentation.

The layout at Camp 4 had certain combinations that I did not see in any other camp. From the stump to the flat car at Camp 4, logs advanced by four methods:

From its stump, a log was yarded onto a skidroad where it was coupled with other logs into a turn of four to ten logs, depending on their sizes. The turn was then pulled over the skidroad by a road donkey and pushed onto the narrow-gauge railroad. The railbed was planked, with the rails higher than the planks so the logs would not fall off.

A little locomotive then took the turn from the road donkey and dragged it to the pond where it was uncoupled. The separate logs were pulled into the water by another donkey.

A pond man with a pike pole[38] sorted the logs by size and length and placed them parallel to a timber ramp. The logs were rolled up the timber ramp onto the top of flatcars with the help of a ginpole[39] and loading donkey.

---

[38] *A long-handled tool for moving logs on water, similar to a peavey.*
[39] *A ginpole was a supported pole that had a pulley or block and tackle on its upper end to lift loads.*

CHAPTER 12

When San Francisco Burned

N OT MANY DAYS HAD PASSED AT CAMP 4 after I arrived before I was fully equipped as a Puget Sound lumberjack and the newness of my working apparel had disappeared. I was as grimy as the other fellows — I was one of them.

The fun of kidding me about my clothes and of my being "Just from the East, eh?" had worn off. The weather was growing warmer and dryer. Things just moved along nicely. The wages were good, and I began to like being a lumberjack, though looking into my future, it did not arouse much enthusiasm.

But, on April 18, 1906, logging on the Pacific Coast received a stimulating shot. Only a war or a catastrophe could so suddenly and effectively cause such a change in an industry.

On that day, San Francisco was destroyed by an earthquake, then fire. The city had to be rebuilt. For a few days the news was just news. Too bad for San Francisco. The railroad engineer brought the information and we talked about it. The newspapers, especially the *Seattle Post-Intelligencer*, published a great deal about it. Lumberjacks, however, did not read newspapers for news. The venereal disease advertisements of the pink section were more interesting to some of them.

The ruins of San Francisco, still smoldering after the fires that followed the 1906 earthquake, taken from the tower of the Union Ferry Building, and looking southwest down Market Street.

By July 4, the really important news began to come in. Camps that had been closed for months, sometimes years, were re-opening. Sawmills of all sizes were being built along the railroads, and others were being enlarged and improved.

Shipping docks were put in order and enlarged for extensive coastal shipping — especially for lumber. Ballard's shingle mills boomed as soon as cedar arrived from the camps. Anything to get timber to the mills and lumber to San Francisco. Many longshoremen found work in logging camps; adventurous lumberjacks went sailing temporarily, traveling to San Francisco and its high wages. As regular lumberjacks left, logging-camps hired everyone they could attract at high wages, and the wages skyrocketed.

Daily wages for skidroad men jumped from $2.25 to $3.50 a day. Fallers' wages went from $2.75 to $4.50 and up. Donkey engineers could now earn $6 rather than $4. Loaders wages rose to $150.00 a month, plus board, from $4 a day.

Wages for other jobs increased correspondingly. Lumberjacks were on the move. They shifted among districts, particularly between Puget Sound and Grays Harbor.

And the machinery changed. By the fall of 1906 and early 1907, the line-horse had disappeared from yarding technique, and the donkey winch had taken its place. Some cables were made thicker and stronger. More powerful yarder and road donkeys were manufactured, and the rigging became stout and heavy.

As the July 4 vacation approached, there was more than the usual unrest among the lumberjacks.

When the logging train pulled away from Camp 4 the Saturday afternoon before July 4, I stayed behind and induced Ole to remain with me. Uncle Fred St. Clair went to Buckley for few days and returned to camp broke and shaky.

Ole and I walked through the cuttings, up the old skidroads, and into the forest. We went fishing. (The big ones got away.) While alone on one walk, I came across an abandoned homesteader's clearing and crumbled shack. In the small clearing lay felled, but not bucked trees, mostly firs. There was not even a garden spot. It was apparent that the homestead laws of the United States had not been remotely complied with and the title to the homestead had been perfected by perjured statements — tactics of the timber barons.

Before the week was over a few lumberjacks — those who had not gotten further than Buckley, Enumclaw, or Wilkinson, began to drift back to camp. When the log train pulled in on Monday morning, Frank Elliot had only a skeleton crew.

Of the lumberjacks who did not return was the skidroad hooktender who had been in the same crew as I.

Every day for more than three months I had seen skidroad building in all of its phases, so Frank Elliot promoted me from skidroad man to skidroad hooktender where, with the help of Uncle Fred St. Clair and Anton Benson, I got along. My wages increased from two dollars and twenty-five cents a day to five dollars a day. By actual experience and with skilled supervision and instruction, I learned to build skidroads.

My mind was on my bank account.

CHAPTER 13

Fire!

THE FORESTS WERE VERY DRY in July, August, and September, and the debris in cutover land was perfect tinder. The fire hazard from the wood-burning donkeys was great and, although aware of their responsibilities, loggers were careless — or indifferent. They could not learn that the donkey engines' spark arresters were often defective.

One, hot, dry mid-September night in 1906, a fire broke out among the logs near a yarder. Somebody woke during the night and through the bunkhouse's slanting skylight saw the yellow sky. The foreman raised a cry, and the crew rushed to the scene of the conflagration, which had already made great headway. Probably under no other condition were men so helpless to fight and try to control and extinguish a forest fire. Everything was perfect for a catastrophe.

When the firs were felled, they had stripped trees standing nearby of their branches and crushed all the underbrush. The branches had been cut and piled in windrows or dropped alongside logs. Pitch-saturated chips from the undercuts lay in piles at the base of stumps and under the butt logs with their exposed pitch seams. Fluid pitch had seeped from the tops of the stumps, flowed down and dried on the bark. The cuts at the ends of the logs were filled with drying pitch. Each conk that had been knocked off a standing tree left a hole, potentially a little furnace too high to reach.

In layers, from the ground up, lay humus; dry leaves; large, dead ferns; branches and crushed small trees; sawed logs steeped with pitch; splintered chunks lying across the stumps and logs; loose, dry bark; and, finally, fine debris that had floated over everything when the trees fell. And among all that stood the tall, crumbly-barked firs, and the dead snags with dry conks still clinging to them. Fuel could not have been arranged more efficiently for burning.

The lumberjacks fought the ground fires and the large embers that scattered from the branches. The flaming widowmakers fell or shot like meteors.

The intense heat kept the men too far from the fires to check the flames. They struggled to create firebreaks ahead of the fire under the rising and billowing smoke. But fire breaks were useless: as the men fought the fire in front and cleared treacherous embers behind, other fires sprang up in the conks high in the firs.

First whiffs of smoke from the conks, then little flames, and then the whole top of the fir flared and the smoke whirled and the treetops swayed.

The fallers rushed to those burning trees. They chopped

and sawed and fought the sparks dropping from the conks and from the floating, burning boughs. When flames struck a dry snag with bark on it, the flame clung and licked and shot to the top, spreading into other firs.

Large sparks shot by, and the blasting-furnace-like air struck and burned.

It was impossible to make a firebreak among the logs. The great weight of the logs and chunks of trees pressed the debris tightly against the humus. The debris burned and flames covered the logs. The bark crackled. Shooting sparks flared. Black smoke choked.

Ahead, in the wind pressed by the fire, the men lined the railroad and skidroads. They picked the dry fuel from along the rails and from between the ties and threw it back into the fire. They tore up the planks between the rails to save the earth-tamped ties. The fallers watched for burning conks and dry, pitchy stubs among the standing timber.

Suddenly, without warning, the fallers saw little tongues of flame on the other side of the firebreak, the narrow railroad grade, and the skidroad. A little smoke whiffed from the side of a fir. It curled and flared, floated and rose with the wind.

The fallers rushed to the fir and methodically and cautiously made their notches, then climbed up on the spring-boards. They glanced up and chopped, glanced up and chopped. Watching for widowmakers, they made the undercut.

The air darkened and the wind blew harder over them.

They sawed in danger, but without fear. The other men stood by where the fir would crash — waiting to pounce upon the fires in the conk holes. The wood at the undercut cracked.

"Timber –er –er –er!"

The men backed to safety, still tense to rush to the tree.

The fir vibrated and swayed. The flames flared and the cyclonic smoke rose, rolled, and merged into the sky.

The fir crashed to the ground. As it struck, it lunged, and the air folded over it.

The flames burst up again as the crowns of nearby trees swayed and flung their fine needles into the frightful wall of flames. Small branches burned in the swirling flames below. The wind whipped into the debris and scattered and drove myriads of sparks into the forest.

The men rushed the fallen fir and shoveled clay over the blazing conks. New little fires flared at the edges where the men worked, burned along the ground, and spread.

Just ahead, another whiff of smoke high up in another fir. Flames jetted out and, fanned by the wind, enveloped the bark and lashed and licked up the trunk. The fire reached into the crown and in the darkness of the swirling smoke, flared like great flashes of lightening.

Everywhere conks burned and the fire spread. Flames licked and consumed their way into the deep-green trees.

The men were hot, dry, and sooty. The fire was so terrific, they abandoned it and fled. They dodged little fires, repelled falling sparks, covered their faces with their hands and arms. As they fled, they turned and saw fire among the logs, like a vast furnace.

Flames flashed from treetop to treetop — fir, hemlock, spruce, and cedar burned. Then the flames shortened and disappeared in the smoke. The embers smoldered.

Suddenly, a blast of air struck again. The embers burst into flames. Through tornado-like smoke, the flames shot out like the shining bayonets of fantastic giants charging their foes.

The crew reached the clearing where the logs were yarded. The land was denuded. The fire charged. The flames lapped and reached, forming a long, solid wall. They hesitated, then flared and ran along the skidroads. Churned debris and slender roots that had been bared and lacerated by the yarded logs burned.

The fire ate into the windrows and moved toward Camp 4. As it advanced into clearer ground, it slackened. The flames shortened, and here and there they slowly vanished but left the embers to smolder and smoke. Finally, the fire reached old logged-over ground, which had burned before and destroyed every living thing. The crew had stopped it.

Retreating, the fire swung to the edge of the timber, where, like a great unyielding ravenous beast, it continued to lick and devour.

Men do not extinguish forest fires like this one. Such fires burn themselves out when there is nothing left to consume or when rains, in their benevolence, extinguish them. But in the distance, the fire continued to crackle and burn, filling the air with smoke so dark that, even by morning, the sun was a dull yellow disk like a pale moon on a misty night. The smoke settled in the valley, obscuring the mountain sides and the top of Mt. Rainier.

The fire left behind piles of embers that smoked. And among the burned trunks still standing, little fires smoldered where the conks had been. The conk holes were protected from the rain, and those little fires burned into the winter in defiance of the damp air.

The crew assembled at the camp to helplessly watch the continued destruction of a large area of magnificent forest. Tornado-like smoke billowed up through the great firs, rolling over the green tops. At the camp, the entire crew filled buckets and tubs with water from the pond, improvised ladders and climbed to the tops of the buildings. They watched for falling sparks — boards and cedar shakes were perfect tinder.

In the distance, smoke rolled over the mountains.

CHAPTER 14

A Woodrat in Camp 3

M cDougal & Jackson built four camps to log timber under contract with the St. Paul & Tacoma Lumber Company, and all of the camps were in operation before 1906. By the time I arrived, logging had finished in Camps 1 and 2, and they were permanently abandoned. At Camp 3, the timber was logged on the most level ground, and then the crew moved to Camp 4. After logging the timber on the easiest ground there, operations resumed in Camp 3 on steep terrain badly lacerated by gullies and valleys.

McDougal & Jackson were like other loggers: they first removed the timber from the easily logged ground, made good profits, and then lost everything later by logging on the more rugged terrain.

Camp 3 was at the junction of two railroad spurs, one of which curved to the southeast along the base of the steep slope of the mountain and the other that swung to the southwest. The buildings in Camp 3 were similar to those at Camp 4, except they were larger.

The first men transferred to Camp 3 included the skidroad

donkey crew of which I was hooktender, the skidroad swampers, and the skidroad laborers. In all, there were about twenty-five men. Later, the fallers and the buckers at Camp 4 also transferred.

When we re-opened Camp 3, it was bare, desolate, and depressing. At first, I felt as though we were taking over a tiny ghost town. The only redeeming feature while we waited for the rest of the crew from Camp 4 was the good food. That was made possible because of the small number of men. The cook had time to prepare special dishes for us.

Camp 3 had been built to accommodate an unusually large crew. There were two big bunkhouses, and we could bunk in either. The men who spoke foreign languages grouped together in one, and Uncle Fred St. Clair, Old Anton Benson, and I with the five or six men with whom we shared a common language took bunks in the other. Camp 3 was two miles nearer to Buckley than Camp 4, so every night enough of the fellows went to town to cause the camp to seem almost deserted. Had it not been for Old Anton and the cribbage games we played nearly every evening, it would not have been possible for me to stay. Sundays were the worst.

Each bunk was like a little cell with the door open. The dusty cobwebs looked like clouds, and the bunks were infested with bedbugs, roaches and spiders. But no lice.

There was no bullcook, so the care and cleanliness of our quarters was left entirely to us. Anything that could be done to better our comfort was left to each man's whim, and no one had any whim except to endure things as we found them.

The big bellied wood stove was too large at times, then too small at others. When the penetrating, damp cold began to make itself felt, a great fire was necessary, but when the fire died down, the cold mountain air quickly took over.

The whole place was so miserable, I decided to build a shack that I could occupy alone.

About two miles up the branch line sat the remains of Camp 2. It had been abandoned long enough for the buildings to collapse. But the lumber was in good condition, so I borrowed the pushcar from the railroad section foreman and with the help of my two old friends, I transported salvaged lumber. The lumber consisted of ordinary rough boards that I used for the walls and the floor. I constructed the gabled roof with cedar shakes. The rafters, beams, and joists were made of small poles.

Near the storehouse I found a large, rusty, iron, oil drum. Lee Abbott, our blacksmith, cut a hole near the bottom for a door and a hole in the top for a tin stovepipe. My fuel was chunks of pitchy bark that I peeled off stumps or picked up in the cuttings nearby. In Buckley, I bought a small kerosene lamp for which I made a crescent shaped reflector from a gallon tomato can.

A two-inch iron pipe had been laid from a small reservoir up the side of the mountain to provide water for the camp. That water pipe passed close to the door of my shack, so one Sunday,

Lee Abbott came and connected a quarter-inch water pipe to the main line and extended it into my shack. In one corner of the shack I constructed a bunk and padded it with fine twigs stripped from cedar boughs. A small table made of box boards and covered with a piece of old oilcloth stood at the one-pane window. I had two round chunks of wood for stools. Near the

Landing, camp buildings, and the logging crew at Camp 3, 1907. The little building with the window at the top center is the author's shack. (From the author's collection.)

door was an apple crate for my washstand and a box above it for a cabinet. Except for the van, my shack was the only building with a door that could be locked. The regular lumberjacks would not have disturbed anything, but occasionally a knight-of-the-road came on a side trip to camp.

Alone in my shack, I could read without much interference. Nearly all the literature that I read was in magazines that were considered particularly good. I recall especially Metropolitan, Outlook, and National Geographic. National Geographic was quite an attraction. Some of the boys liked the pictures. They also liked the comfort of my shack. I had only one book, *Human Nature and Social Order* by Professor Thomas Cooley of the University of Michigan. The book had been a gift from a schoolmate for my 1904 high school graduation. I wrote little. The only corresponding that I did was the occasional letter to my grandmother who had raised me and whom I adored. Grandmother wrote in French, which I read well but could not write, so I wrote to her in English, which some friends translated for her.

During the time Camp 3 was unoccupied, the woodrats had taken possession. They seemed to be everywhere under the floors and the lower bunks. The large piles of rotten rubbish and empty tin cans were hideouts. After the crew had retired and the lights were out, those woodrats jumped, cavorted, and sneaked into bedding more boldly than I had ever known them to do. And nothing was safe from being dragged away. We tried to trap them with deadfall traps, but we made even more noise, and it seemed to intensify their boldness.

I had fitted the boards and shakes of my shack as tightly as possible, and it seemed to me that not a woodrat could enter except through the open door. I was always inside when it was open. One Sunday night after I had returned from Buckley where I had spent the day, I was rudely reminded that my meticulous caution had been in vain. I had previously pushed a small box of apples under my bunk and covered it with a loose inch-thick board. Having settled myself for an evening's relaxation, I dragged out my box to get an apple. The lid was pushed to one side and the box was empty. I looked around. I could see no apples.

Carrying my lamp in one hand, I searched for a hole in the floor and walls. Everything was all right: no hole was large enough for an apple to pass through. I was certain that a woodrat was the culprit. I put out the light. There was dead silence — woodrats will not move if they hear humans, except if those humans are snoring. Woodrats seem to understand the meaning of snores.

Alert, I waited for what seemed a long time, then I heard light thump — thump — thumps. There was silence, then more thumps. Quickly I re-lit my lamp and turned it in the direction of the thumps. A gray woodrat! The woodrat jumped to a crossbeam and followed it to the wall and my box shelf. There, to my astonishment, were my apples piled neatly against the back of the box. Over the top of the pile was that woodrat, wiggling its nose and ears, and blinking its large, round, bulging eyes.

Slyly I got a stick to put an end to that nuisance. Carefully, I moved an apple. The woodrat slunk back. I pushed the end of my stick in the direction of its head to strike. It shifted its head.

I struck! And hit the back of the box. A jump of gray, a repulsive thud on my head, a scoot, and the woodrat was gone. It had gained entrance by tearing the heavy paper from over a large knothole at the back of my bunk.

CHAPTER 15

Christmas in Seattle

THE DENSE, COLD, AND DISAGREEABLE Oregon mist of winter had begun to moderate when I started to work for McDougal & Jackson in March 1906. The fog over the region was dispersing earlier each morning. Mt. Rainier was more visible through the breaking clouds. The snow line on the Cascade and Olympic mountains set off clearly the vast, deep green forests on their slopes and in the valleys. Then soothing spring — too short — followed by the oppressively hot, dry days of July and August. Seasonal forest fires left much scorched, charred timber and sooty logs. And then, too soon, the return of the rain. Chilling, snow-flaked rain. Mud and more mud. The dragging hours of late fall and winter days. Then, finally Christmas, and a week's vacation away from the educational, but rotten, environment.

I would be going to a large seaport city — the kind of city that I had never experienced and of which I had heard the worst. I was going to Tacoma or Seattle.

I listened to the crew animatedly discuss plans and reminisce about the kinds of recreation they had enjoyed — relating past experiences to be renewed in saloons, brothels, and cribs. A few had homes or family connections near Buckley.

Nine months of continuous, unvarying drabness, discomfort, hard work, and monotonous living was as much as I could endure without respite. To detach myself from that atmosphere and to recapture the feeling of cleanliness and the sense of decency was imperative. I began to realize that physically and psychologically, a man may deteriorate rapidly, and when he realizes his state, his future may already be irreparably damaged and redirected.

Everybody would go somewhere — even if only for a day. Logging operations ceased at noon on the Saturday before Christmas. After dinner, we tried to clean ourselves of mud and soot with cold water from the creek or, for the more fastidious, with water in tin cans heated on the big, bunkhouse stove. We put on our best clothes, which were not much.

At about two o'clock, we climbed onto the muddy and bark-covered floors of the flatcars. Winding down the mountain, the log train carried us to Buckley where the crew would disperse to Seattle, Tacoma, Everett, and the smaller towns.

Most talked about Tacoma and Seattle — mostly about Tacoma — and what sort of entertainment was available in those cities. All the talk was sordid. But was it true or exaggerated? I had seen a bit of Seattle, including the waterfront and the Skid Road. I was anxious to see more of the city, so I decided to go there. Even if some of Seattle was rotten, it must also have that which was pleasant.

In camp the crew got along well together. There appeared to be some close companionships. But after they arrived in town, their friendships quickly disintegrated. By the time the evening train to Seattle pulled in at Buckley, a number of the fellows were talkative and pompous, while others were so slobbery drunk that they clung to whomever they could and staggered to the depot. A few remained behind, having gone to the little red house with four broads[40] down by the bridge over the river.

There they were, a group of nearly one hundred men who had worked together from a few days to several months, whose behavior had leveled off to a common pattern while in camp, but which now had crumbled, each revealing himself in the raw. Before leaving Buckley, I saw that some of the short-timers in the camp had boozed or blackjacked away their money, and I soon became aware that I was an attraction for moochers.

The train stopped and the lumberjacks who remained were herded into a special coach for lumberjacks and their caulked boots at the back of the train, something every passenger train on Puget Sound had.

The occupation of lumberjack carried a stigma that was imprinted on every one of them. Good or bad, they were a race apart, but necessary, tolerated, and exploitable.

The lumberjack coach was drab, its windows moldy. The

---

[40] *The use of "broad" to mean prostitute originated in the early 20th century.*

conductor stood at one side of the steps and the brakeman at the other. The second brakeman stood between the coaches to prevent any of the fellows from going through to the good coaches.

When the train pulled out, each coach started with a jerk, but the last one jerked so hard that those of us who were sitting were slammed into the hardwood seatbacks. Those standing were thrown reeling in the aisles.

The rain began to beat harshly against the opaque windows, blurring and streaming as the train rumbled and clacked through the countryside. Form and substance vanished, and the stinking coach became smellier.

"Puyallup, Puyallup –up –up –up," called the brakeman as he aroused the dozing lumberjacks, examining the tickets that were fumbled to him. "Change cars for Tacoma."

While the Tacoma passengers were stumbling out, I sneaked into the day coach ahead.

Since those days, I have thought that nowhere on earth could nights be more intensely black than they are during rainy season on Puget Sound. The ride was monotonous. Anxious to reach Seattle, I glanced at my watch frequently.

Eventually, the coaches jammed together with loud clangs, the train began to coast and the locomotive's whistling grew longer. Raucous whistles recognizable as those of steamboats informed us that we were entering Seattle. The train screeched to a stop among the inadequate lights of the passenger depot. The ceaseless rain poured its chill against the windows. Outside, Elliott Bay was dark.

The little blue railroad depot was located on the waterfront at the base of the long, broad, curved slope to which much of Seattle clings. The depot was like the ones that may be seen in dying towns in some of the unhappily homesteaded acres of the dry west and in Lake Superior country that have been devastated by lumbering. People shouldered and bumped through the narrow doors. The odor was worse than in the coach.

Without delay, I ventured out to find a room for the night. The fellows had suggested some places on Skid Road. I had been there upon my first arrival in Seattle, but now it was night.

I had never before been in a situation like this, and I was frightened. The hurrying people dispersed so quickly and the poorly lighted streets appeared so empty that it gave me a feeling of abandonment. No one gave notice to others — everybody for himself. Inquiries for direction or information were met with a grunt or complete indifference. Crossing every alley made me jumpy. Dressed like a lumberjack, I could not rent a room in a better part of the city, so I walked for what seemed miles along the waterfront. Later, I learned it was only a short distance.

Dim, cobwebbed lights in dusky hole-like stairways — that was the best I could see, and the hour was late. Tiny rooms, each with a small unkempt bed, a wiggly chair, bare floor, and faded, torn curtains. In contrast, a bunkhouse was a luxury. I finally accepted a room and went to bed with the bugs. I stayed there all day Sunday.

On Sunday morning before daylight as I walked down the narrow tomb-like hallway, a witchy head poked out of a door and a scraggly hand beckoned to me. The first two nights of my vacation in Seattle were spent in a house that catered to transient whores.

The first night of my vacation I had retired while the city's waterfront seethed with life. The following Monday morning I ventured out early before it had roused itself. The area between the wharves — where steamers, tugs, and fishing boats were tied — and the business section of the city was a veritable no-man's land.

Hurrying along the sidewalk in the thick fog, my damp, cold turkey — I had left my nice suitcase in camp — chafing my legs and increasing in weight, I glanced apprehensively at every door, alley, and gloomy opening.

The meager, flickering light from the water's edge dimly lit the gray, low, shabby buildings — many of them with sagging roofs of decaying lumber.

Down the way, lighted windows in the shops and eating places assured me that I was near the Great Northern Railroad depot. Raucous boat whistles from the harbor grew louder, and the outlines of sheds, storehouses, and boats became discernible. Murky Elliott Bay grew grayer.

More and more men stumbled from the alleys and hurried across the tracks to merge into groups on the docks like great

Seattle wharves and waterfront on the left, 1906.

beetles returning to their hills after a foray. They were the long-shoremen in the peculiar stride of their occupation.

Iron wheels of vans and carts rattled over the waterfront's uneven planks and the cobble stones of the narrow streets and alleys.

I stepped into the receded entrance of a building front when bright lights flashed on and the windows shone attractively illuminated. Setting down my turkey to rest and get my bearings, I was shocked as I straightened up and beheld again the sickening exhibits of distorted models of the diseased human reproductive organs. At once a man with a rat-profiled face opened the door, stepped out, and began to explain the display.

"Want to see the doctor?"

The garish-colored wax figures and models in the window made me retch. I had seen the effects of gonorrhea and syphilis in a few lumberjacks. I snapped up my turkey and ran.

I entered the first good men's clothing store that I saw and bought an entire outfit. I also bought a leather suitcase. I packed my things into the new suitcase and discarded the dirty sack that had served me so well since leaving camp.

After exiting the store, I meandered along streets until I located what appeared to be a decent and moderately priced hotel, The Occidental. Though not nice inside — the room was dirty — it seemed good enough for a lumberjack.

By the time that I had loitered about the hotel and neighborhood to get my bearings, the evening was turning to dusk. Since those were Christmas shopping days, the stores remained open late and the streets were beautifully lighted. The crowds were large and vigorous. Although rain was falling hard, people stayed out dressed in rubber sailor hats, coats, or capes. I ventured into the street; but soon I was aware that my new suit would be wet, so I went back to the hotel, read a paper, chatted with strangers, and went to bed. I felt safe and slept soundly.

My first Tuesday in Seattle started early. During the previous day I had seen better hotels, and I began to make comparisons. My room faced a gloomy alley and a brick wall.

After my toilet, I left my suitcase at the front desk and

went out to look for breakfast. The rain had faded to thick mist.

The more attractive restaurants were still closed. Only low-class ones that catered to the dock men, sailors, laborers, and lumberjacks were open. If they were good enough for those fellows, they ought to be all right for me. But as I watched men going in and out, I grew disgusted with the atmosphere — nearly all the patrons showed the effects of a hard night.

I selected a restaurant. The window display was appetizing, and the prices suited my purse. Ham and eggs were fifteen cents, doughnuts were two for a nickel, with all the coffee one could drink included. The place was clean, and the food smelled good. When my order came, I discovered the reason for the low prices. The doughnuts were miniature, and the eggs were about the size of two egg yolks. The coffee tasted like water from reboiled coffee grounds. There were many of those restaurants throughout that section of Seattle. They were gyp joints owned by hard-faced people.

When I stepped out on the street, the soupy fog had begun to clear, and the white disk of sun was visible over the Cascade Mountains. The raucous steamboat whistles along the waterfront and in Elliott Bay were a constant sound.

As the forenoon wore on, I began to worry about the safety of my new suitcase. I hurried to The Occidental Hotel. By the time that I arrived, the fog had disappeared from the high section of the city, which loomed beautiful in contrast to the dirty waterfront.

With my new outfit, I felt at ease as I climbed up the hillside and the streets became cleaner and nicer.

I was looking for a better hotel. I meandered along, window-shopping and enjoying the rapidly increasing crowd and traffic. Street cars rattled along the hillside and a few cars pulled by a stout cable climbed the hill. From street intersections, I could see quite a distance into the face of the city. I noticed a number of large rooming houses, apartments, and a nice hotel, all far enough removed from the busy section of the city to permit rest and easy access to the waterfront, theaters, and city market.

Prices at The Holland, a white brick hotel, appeared to be within my range, so I went in. The hotel was beautiful, seven stories high, and from my room on the top floor I had an excellent view over the harbor, Elliott Bay, and the mountains.

I had made good wages, so I had enough money to insure myself decent comfort during my vacation. Although I had been working and living in a rough environment, I was able to remain aloof from the crude men with whom I had worked. No one seemed to suspect, or care, that I was a lumberjack. All that day I lounged about the hotel, reading the Sunday papers and engaging in conversations with various persons.

I had never been fortunate enough to see a good play, so after supper I strolled to a street with large stores with attractive window displays and theaters. Not caring for vaudeville, I sought a theater in which I might see a play. After looking at the advertisements of two or three theaters, I chose The Grand where a stock company was performing Romeo and Juliet. The actors' performances were so fascinating, I saw the play again the following night.

My week in Seattle was pleasant and educational. I saw all that I could. At the large city market, I bought fruit, such as grapes and apples, which I munched as I meandered along. I spent much time in the large city library and along the waterfront where the docked ocean steamers fascinated me. I took a trip to Bremerton, the United States naval base, where it was a thrill to board the old battleship *Oregon* of Spanish-American War fame.

The Holland was such a restful hostelry that had it not been for my restlessness, nearly all of my week would have been spent there lounging about, especially on the built-in balcony on the second floor.

Early in the afternoon of the day following my registration at The Holland, I discovered a large mezzanine on the second floor. There were beautiful pictures on the walls, and the carpets and chairs were so relaxing. As I was enjoying myself there I noticed a group of young people at the farthest end of the floor from me. They were talking animatedly while reading from manuscripts as though they were rehearsing. The group was the stock company of The Grand, preparing their next play. Quietly, I moved to the most secluded part of the mezzanine where I sat during the whole rehearsal.

The rehearsals were every afternoon, so for three after-noons at about two o'clock, I went to my vantage point. I was the only spectator, and none of the actors seemed to care.

After the third afternoon, several of the actors walked by me. One young actress whom I recognized as Pinky Mollaly (her stage name) smiled at me and said, "Hello!" Boy, did that delight me. That evening I was back to see Romeo and Juliet.

Every day as the week progressed, I did the same thing and went to the same places: waterfront, University of Washington, library, market, window-shopping, and, of course, listening to the rehearsals at The Holland.

Each day Miss Pinky became friendlier and friendlier. Some of the other cast members began to say, "Hello."

After the rehearsal one afternoon while I was sitting entranced, Miss Pinky passed my way and she engaged me in conversation. She asked me my occupation and when I told her I was just a lumberjack she appeared surprised and smiled. There was much loveliness in her personality. I told her of my plans to go to college and where I wished to go. She asked other questions and she spoke encouragingly. Some of the other actors and actresses went by and nodded and smiled.

I told Miss Pinky how much I enjoyed the play and of course the acting of the leading lady, whom I thought was charming. She had that indefinable something that I would always remember. I excitedly told Miss Pinky that it would be the delight of my life to meet the leading lady, but of course I was just a lumberjack. Miss Pinky smiled, and I think she winked.

After the rehearsal broke up, Miss Pinky turned to join her friend who was approaching and smiling. As I stepped back so as not to be obtrusive, Miss Pinky asked me to wait. In one of the pleasantest incidents of my life I was introduced to a great actress, and an unforgettable lady — Eileen May.[41]

The following Sunday I returned to the logging camp near Buckley for six months of snow, rain, mud, and hard labor, but with an understanding that not all prominent people are snobs.

---

[41] *Wilfred named his second child Eileen Mae.*

CHAPTER 16

From Stump to Mill

BY MID-SUMMER OF **1906,** McDougal & Jackson was nearing the end of its operation near Buckley. Camp 4 was abandoned, and Camp 3's crew had been reduced to the minimum requirements for cleanup. Uncle Fred St. Clair, skidroad foreman; Old Anton Benson, skidroad swamper and faller, as well as cribbage champion; Abe Rutherford; and Ole, the Swede, had all left. Ole was the only one I would see again.

My job as hooktender was about to close, so when the crew climbed onto the flatcars the afternoon that we left for our July 4th vacation, I took all my belongings to Buckley where I boarded a train for Tacoma.

I had heard that wages were higher in Grays Harbor country, and up-to-date equipment and methods were being used. I had also heard that the Oregon mist was too continuous and the ground was too rough, not mountainous but a devil's washboard. But the wages were appealing, and that was all important. So I spent my week in Tacoma and then proceeded to Aberdeen, which was one of the principal cities in the Grays Harbor area. In Aberdeen, I found work as a loader in the camp of

S.E. Slade Lumber Company near Elma.

Though I had seen thousands of logs loaded onto flatcars, I had never loaded any. But relying on my experience as a hooktender, knowledge of the power of donkeys, and familiarity with the equipment needed to move large, long logs, I was confident I could do it.

Logging was different there and taxed the knowledge and ingenuity of the most skilled lumberjacks. Joe Beledeau, a big French Canadian and one of the most skilled loggers, was camp superintendent. Mike Doyle, a little gray-haired gentleman who was proud of the shamrock, was the strawboss of the side[42] on which I worked.

Fir, cedar, hemlock, and the famous Grays Harbor spruce grew in the area. The timber there was not large, but it was uniform and exceptionally thick.

Let us go back to late fall 1907 and follow a log from its stump to the S.E. Slade Lumber Mill in Aberdeen.

The rain has been falling steadily for days. We work in the rain or we do not work at all. Abrasions in the ground have turned to mud, while gouges are full of water on top of which ice forms at night. Moss from the trees falls and sticks to our faces and hands. The rain oozes through our felt hats. In desperation, we work bareheaded. Our thick, blue shirts are soaked and heavy and clinging. Our tinpants are caked with

---

[42] *The crew and equipment for a yard outfit. A camp might have more than one side and, thus, more than one yard.*

The crew at S.E. Lumber Company's camp near Elma. Note that the ground landing is almost level with the flatcars. The author is on the far right. (From the author's collection.)

clay, our leather gloves slimy, and our feet slop in our flooded shoes, out of which the water squishes as we work. Large snowflakes float down and melt slowly. We are not cold enough to freeze, just cold enough to suffer.

I am the hooktender of the side where Mike Doyle is foreman. He promoted me to hooktender a few days after I started to load.

My crew includes the rigging-slinger, two chokermen, a barker, a sniper, the chaser, the signalpunk, the yard donkey engineer, and the fireman.

The setting is a thousand feet higher than the landing. The

logs lie among broken trees and behind stumps. They are in places that make them difficult to yard, plus they must be sorted so they can be made into a good turn.

I carefully inspect the area. I must take advantage of the logs' positions as they lay among the stumps. The best way to start logs is straight ahead, and they are generally felled parallel to each other. If I can, I must move and set the yard donkey so that the logs are yarded uphill. No matter how steep a hill, the yarder will be able to pull the logs up. Uphill yarding is the only way to keep the logs under control as they are dragged. I have yarded logs up a steep hill or mountain side, then sent them downhill over a skidroad.

We must move the yard donkey from its old setting to a new one. While I select the new setting, the rigging-slinger unfastens an anchor line that has been holding the donkey to a big stump; the fireman fills the firebox so there will be a full head of steam. The chokermen and chaser load the equipment onto the front of the donkey's sled. The signalpunk takes down his signal wire, which is attached to a whistle on the yard donkey. We are ready to move the yard donkey.

The donkey slides awkwardly toward the new setting by means of its own power, using a cable fastened to a stump. Chunks, uprooted stumps, stiff stubs of roots, and culled logs protrude in the path of the advancing donkey. The great sled shifts and jerks from side to side. Every move it makes must be slow and under my control. I stand on the front of the sled or

A heavy bullblock, date unknown but probably later than when Wilfred worked on Puget Sound, because bullblocks in his day were anchored low to the ground.

jump off and run ahead. At the jerk of my hand, the engineer stops the donkey, and the line — the cable pulling the donkey — slumps to the ground. We rest while the fireman puts wood in the firebox.

On we go. The donkey dips into holes, rises again, tips to one side, skids past stumps and trees, breaks and uproots small trees, and pushes everything out of its way.

After much maneuvering, the donkey slides into place in

the new setting and the sled is anchored by cable to a large stump or tree behind it. Next, we pull a split or conky log near the firebox for the fireman to cut for fuel.

A hundred feet or so ahead of the donkey, the rigging-slinger anchors a bullblock[43] low on a sturdy fir stump near the ground that can withstand the jarring and tremendous pull by the donkey as the moving logs hit trees and stumps and tear through the trash on the ground.

Next, I select the trees to anchor the haulback.[44] The rigging-slinger, chokermen, and I each shoulder a haulback block, walk to the selected trees and hang the blocks as high as we can reach standing on stumps or logs. The haulback must run freely.

With the haulback blocks set, the yarding crew gathers at the donkey wearing leather gloves to protect their hands from broken wire in the cable. Taking the spliced end of the haulback, I trample over the logs and chunks and branches to the first haulback block, the others following. We climb down the valley and up again, down and up, and on and on. When I reach the haulback block, I close the cable in the block.

I continue on, setting the cable in the other haulbacks, pulling the cable harder and harder with the crew behind me

---

[43] *A large block, or pulley, weighing about one hundred to two hundred pounds. The block was anchored to a large tree or stump by a heavy cable strap.*

[44] *A long steel cable used to pull other cables. The cables that moved the logs were too heavy for the lumberjacks, so the cables were hauled from wherever they had ended up — a skidroad, say — back to the forest with the haulback cable.*

pulling, too. We pull and sweat and grunt until we are almost exhausted, until we feel our guts bulging out. There was never anything in eastern logging that was as hard as pulling a haulback. This effort continues until the haulback is back to the bullblock anchored to the big stump in front of the yarder.

A chokerman attaching cables to a log. The author is at the far right. (From the author's collection.)

Sometimes as much as three or four thousand feet of haulback is stretched at one time.

The yarding equipment is set and ready for yarding logs from where they were felled to the skidroad.

While the logs are being yarded, the signalpunk fastens his wire from the donkey whistle to a tree while always staying in sight of the rigging crew. The fireman and the engineer run a water line from the engine to a small pool. If there were no pool, the fireman would need to carry buckets of water to the donkey.

The barker has barked the bellies[45] of the thicker-bark firs; smaller firs, spruce, cedar, and hemlock are not barked. The sniper snipes[46] the front end of the logs.

The first logs that are yarded move easily, but as the yarding extends further into the woods, the gouges in the earth become deeper, more stumps and trees and chunks of earth block the way. There are more hills down which the logs can slide and go out of control, more swamps and deep waterholes with invisible rocks and roots.

The chokerman's job is to put a choker around the log so when the haulback returns the rigging and cable from the last log yarded, he can hook on the cable. When the rigging arrives, it is attached to the log. I wave my arm and the signalpunk snaps his wire to blow the donkey whistle and signal the engineer.

The log moves slowly. A thousand feet ahead through the trees we see the donkey's spurting smoke and hear it puffing. The rigging-slinger and I follow the log while the chokerman stays behind to prepare the next log.

Reluctantly, the log careens up and down, diving into holes and splashing great sheets of mud, tearing roots, and pil-

---

[45] *The belly is the flattest side of a log on which the log will ride when it is dragged.*
[46] *Rounds the front ends of the logs so they will glance off stumps and other objects and not gouge the ground.*

The skidroad chaser riding his boat. (From the author's collection.)

ing clay, gravel, and trash to the sides. The great yardline vibrates, stretches across low swamps, slackens, dips.

The log gains on the yardline, and the yardline sags. The log smashes against a stump, then rolls over and drags the yardline and tangles it around itself. The log stops and the lines are tight. This is the result of free sliding downhill. We cannot avoid that — this is Grays Harbor country.

The chaser, rigging-slinger, chokerman, and I grab the yardline and brace ourselves. We strain sideways for a few inches of slack, just enough to unhook the cable from the choker around the log. By pulling, chopping branches, and manipulating the line, we unhook and untangle it.

I climb on the stump in front of the log to watch. I raise my hands. Everyone else rushes away — the power of the donkey is enormous, and things might break and fly. The whistle blows three blasts and the yardline moves slowly. The choker crunches into the log's remaining bark and the log begins to slide.

No one talks much while the log is being yarded, only some cursing as it makes or misses trouble. There is no excitement either, just minute calculations and hard work. The cold air and the slush and mud are too unpleasant for fun.

The ordeal of dragging the log continues as impediments are dealt with, the choker and line are shifted, the donkey strains. The log passes a swamp and starts up a steep hill in the direction of the donkey. The ground is well drained. The log is now entirely under control. It will not run, though it still must navigate around stumps and through holes.

At last the yard donkey moves the log into position for the swing donkey, which will pull the log to the skidroad. More logs follow. The dogger couples the logs into a turn so the road donkey can drag them over the skidroad to the landing. As the turn runs along the skidroad, the skidroad chaser follows, riding astride his pigboat,[47] walking, or standing on the logs.

---

[47] *A flat-bottomed, low-sided sled pointed at both ends. It held small equipment and was fastened to the last log of a turn.*

The turn is still a mile from the landing where it will be loaded onto flatcars to be shipped to and dumped into Grays Harbor at the mouth of the Chehalis River.

The skidroad is entirely made of fore-an-afts. Thousands of logs have been dragged over it, and as it approaches the landing, the middle fore-an-afts are worn thin, and clay and trash are piled high on each side, making a deep ditch.

A jerk of the signal wire. Way down the skidroad, the whistle blows, and the road donkey begins to pull the turn. The couplings between the logs tighten, and the roadline stretches and quivers. The head log jumps, and the turn slides up the skidroad.

The turn reaches the top of a ridge. On the other side is a steep grade. If it rushes downhill, the turn might break the line, so a snub donkey has been anchored at the top of the hill to hold the turn as it slides downhill.

The turn reaches the landing, which is constructed of eight parallel logs about 18 inches in diameter. They extend from the flatcars to the skidroad. Loaders pull the logs across the skidroad to the landing and sort them.

The top of the landing is even with the tops of the flatcars but slopes slightly down toward the cars, not enough, though, for the logs to roll out of control.

Loading a car with uniform logs is not difficult, but a load of varying sizes requires planning, and placing the logs and blocking them requires skill. If the logs are not securely set, they will roll off or spill onto the track when the train moves.

After a car is loaded, a handyman hammers a stamp of the S.E. Slade Lumber Company into the end of each log. Now the train crew of the Northern Pacific Railroad couples onto the cars and hauls them to Aberdeen. The lumberjacks are through.

At the mill, the cars are pulled onto a pier over Grays Harbor and rolled into the water.

CHAPTER 17

Another Kind of Vermin

WHILE I WAS ON ONE OF MY SOJOURNS in Seattle in the summer of 1908, I hired out through an employment office to work in a logging camp on the Tacoma & Eastern Railroad. I was told that the camp was in a broad valley at the foot of Mt. Rainier.

I had heard talk about logging conditions up that way — level and gravely ground, uniform big timber, and, of course, easy access to Tacoma. All the yarding was short and direct to the railroad landing — no skidroads with swing donkeys and road donkeys. It was a good place to tend hook. The employment agent was happy that he could sell such a good job. The wages were all right. I was lucky.

From Seattle to Tacoma, then up to Mt. Rainier was quite a journey for a penny-pinching lumberjack. I paid my fare to Tacoma and then boarded the flatcar logging train.

"Where you going?" asked the brakeman as I stood on a flatcar while the train was being pushed up the track.

I glanced at my employment card and shouted back.

"See you tomorrow on the way back!" the brakeman jibed

as he ran along the cars and climbed on.

We passed rusty-railed and weedy spurs and abandoned landings and campsites, traveling through cutover and devastated land.

The car brakes screeched and the couplings slammed, and there I was at a little plank platform.

Near the platform several men stood on the wet ground with their dirty turkeys and rolled blankets.

"What you going to do?" said an irate lumberjack who was dressed in full regalia — felt hat with the front of the brim turned up pirate-like, double-breasted blue shirt, stagged tinpants, and calked shoes.

"Tend hook," I replied as I lowered my turkey.

"To hell you will. We'll be seein' ya in Tacoma — tomorrow," he said.

Others joined with various oaths — mostly with reference to the foreman's maternity.

With a glance I made an appraisal. The camp buildings, scattered along the track, were old and dilapidated. They had been built before the depression of 1907, closed for a year or so, then re-opened. They had been used by unemployed lumberjacks and tramps. Crossing the track, I passed stinky tinpants, rotting clothes, shoes with gaping holes, and ragged blankets. Among the bushes and stumps there were open toilets or just heaps where men had relieved themselves. Under little bough roofs were improvised beds. The humid air reeked with the odor of decaying filth. I retched.

I stood in the entrance of a doorless and cavelike bunkhouse. The interior was draped with cobwebs. Few of the bunks showed recent occupancy. Each had a bit of frayed straw on it that had been gathered into little piles by the woodrats. The floor was like an infrequently cleaned stockyard, and the four skylights were opaque squares. In the middle of the floor, the tin pipe on the big iron stove had collapsed. Something thumped lightly but distinctly on my felt hat, and when I snapped it off little pellets sank into my hair and rolled down my neck and into my clothing. Bedbugs and fleas were so thick, they rained from the ceiling, clung to the cobwebs, and crouched in every crack.

Trembling, I grabbed my turkey and bundled blankets and dashed out under the misty sky.

Standing in front of a small, new shanty was a well-groomed lumberjack. He displayed an air of pompousness — as if he were a lumberjack legend, a Paul Bunyan.

"You're the foreman?" I demanded.

He squared his shoulders. "Right," he said as he slapped his clean gloves into his left hand and stabbed out his right hand. He grinned.

I hated him with deep passion.

A log train passed, then stopped at the siding to couple onto some loaded cars. The outgoing lumberjacks were already decorating the top logs, and as the locomotive whistle tooted, as with disdain, the train pulled out. None of the fellows looked back.

The foreman examined my yellow employment ticket, "Hooktender, eh? Need one. Other fellow just left. A bum, anyway."

Something scooted down my back and my skin twitched.

"How much d'ya pay them guys?" the foreman asked while he was flipping the ticket over and back.

"Three dollars. Must be a good job," I replied. My eyes were blazing. I knew then that he was a rotten chiseler and that he would fire me the next day. He was in cahoots with the employment agent. They split the employment agent's fees. Lumberjacks considered that the vilest conduct.

"Make y'reself ta home." He thumbed in the direction of the bunkhouse. An' there's the cookhouse. Hope ya'll like it here," he said as he grinned. "Dis a swell place."

I tossed my turkey over my shoulder as we started up the track.

"Say, ever work in logging camps around Lake Superior?" the foreman asked.

"Raised there," I replied. "Ever been there?"

"Oh yes. Ran a big camp there," he said as his flushing face revealed his lie.

We sank to a chunk of broken tree where I sat with my chin resting in my cupped hands while the foreman drew his nice gloves through his hands and slapped them on his knees.

"I was a canthook man — a loader — could whirl like this. Like this. See?" He illustrated clumsily. "Come here ta re-open this camp this spring. I'll show those bastards around here how to take out logs. The way we ustta back there." He looked squarely into my eyes as I nodded. I could tell he was a bully and a scissorbill.

"I want to see the work," I said after the foreman apparently became exhausted from bragging. I suspected he realized I did not believe a thing that he said.

A whiff of air compelled us to walk. There were little piles covered with flies all around.

I hopped into a skidroad trail and saw thick, high stumps and clean ground without chunks, a condition necessary for efficient steam powered drag-logging. The skidtrails curved exactly right. Before the depression, some foreman and hooktender had done a good job. They knew their craft. I had not tended hook under more favorable conditions. With some regained enthusiasm, I leaped to the ground and hurried toward the setting.

But I did not go far. The stumps were freshly cut, but they were short, not waist-high and less than half of the diameter of a large log. There were no springboard notches in the stumps. The fallers had stood on the ground to fell those firs. The entire job showed that it had been done by a lumberjack from the east.

Low stumps saved a little timber and they were all right for horse and oxen logging; however, for steam power drag-logging, the value of the timber saved was more than offset by the added cost of yarding.

Upon seeing the yard donkey, I knew at once that it was not powerful enough to yard such timber efficiently, even on level ground.

It was clear that the crew was inadequate and noticeably unskilled.

I studied the yarding until quitting time when I joined the roustabout crew on the way to camp. I was assured that the foreman was a fee-splitter and that if a fellow did not quit in time, he was fired as soon as someone came to take his place.

After supper, which was fair, I went to a large pile of fir boughs, cleared away a place to make my bed and, with the hope of a rainless night, lay down. The fleas soon found me.

The next morning when the cook sounded his gong for breakfast, the chiseler foreman planted himself outside the cookhouse to accost anyone not on the crew — no money, no meal — and if anyone paid, he pocketed the money.

How that foreman got his job and how long he stayed in charge of that camp I do not know. With other victims of a vicious racket, I joined the crowd to decorate the top of the first train to Tacoma.

I had learned that not only bugs are vermin.

CHAPTER 18

The Widowmaker

E ARLY IN THE AUTUMN OF 1908, the financial panic that had started the previous year and so severely disrupted the lumber industry on the Pacific Coast began to subside. During the depression, many of the more skilled lumberjacks had drifted into other occupations, left the region, or settled on small parcels of land in the valleys. Now sawmills and logging camps were reopening, and employment for lumberjacks was increasing.

The need for skilled lumberjacks was enough to absorb those who cared to resume their occupations, but the wages were much reduced. Hooktenders had been paid between five dollars plus board a day to one hundred and fifty dollars plus board a month. Now they were offered from three dollars and fifty cents to four dollars a day, and from those wages paid their board, usually five dollars a week. The unskilled lumberjacks, of whom there were few, and the men who ventured into the industry for the first time received much less. Even at that, those wages were better than what was paid at sawmills or any other kind of work.

Like nearly all other lumberjacks I was on the move to find a better-paying job.

In Seattle, I hired out at an employment office to work for the Port Blakely Mill Company in Camp E about four miles from Matlock in the forests of Mason County, Washington.

The timber that the company owned at Camp E was on level terrain and the soil was generally gravel. There were some small wet places in which spring-maples grew among the firs. Those spring-maples were always dangerous to the men while they were yarding logs because they were so unpredictable. Sometimes if they were cut while they were sprung, the end flew back with great force.

The fir, which was nearly the only useful timber, was uniformly large — two to six feet in diameter — and stood tall and thick. Probably in no area on the Pacific Coast was there a more beautiful and uniformly large stand of Douglas fir.

The level ground, the gravelly and porous soil, the absence of dead trees and windfalls, and the ease with which the railroad was constructed should have combined to make easy and cheap logging. But that was not the case. I never saw, even on the rolling ground about Grays Harbor, nor in the Skykomish Valley in the Cascade Mountains, such destruction and unnecessary waste of timber.

The waste was caused almost entirely by the unskilled fallers and buckers. The wages paid by the Port Blakely Mill Company were less than average and many of the men were

This is the log shown on the cover, which was lost when the train rails spread. The author is the second from the left, standing on the truck with his hand raised. (From the author's collection.)

recent immigrants with no previous experience in big timber. To overcome the bad work of the fallers and buckers, better wages were paid to the two hooktenders, there being two sides operated in the camp.

There were no skidroads at Camp E. The railroad, which cost no more than a skidroad, was extended to the timber.

The largest Douglas fir that I ever saw was at Camp E. Extremely beautiful, it towered like a red sandstone column above the other firs. To fell that tree was like destroying a landmark of nature that could never be replaced.

Although the fallers who felled that fir were not skilled, they seemed to sense a particular responsibility and felled it well. The bucker also did a good job so none of the tree was damaged. There were six logs in the trunk and each one was enough for a carload.

I never derived more satisfaction from a job well done than I did when those six logs were on as many sets of railroad trucks. Every man in camp took pride in it, too. On the Sunday following the yarding of the big butt log, a commercial photographer came to camp and took a picture of some of the crew with it, and also a picture of me standing against the end.

However, timber was plentiful on Puget Sound. When that train with the six logs was on its way to the landing, it was wrecked because the rails spread, and every log with its truck rolled down a short, steep bank. The trucks were unchained and pulled back to the track, but it was impossible to reload the logs, so they were sawed into fuel for the wood-burning locomotive.

Life at Camp E was no different from that in any other logging camp: the same drabness, the same loneliness, the same routine. One evening before Thanksgiving, I went out to supper. The air was cold and the night was intensely depressing. On such a night no one mentioned the rain or the cold. He just felt it. There was so much of both at that time of the year that the fellows seemed to shrink.

The cookhouse was warm, comfortable, and invigorating.

The air was aromatic, and steam floated up from the hot food. The men did not converse — that was the rule — except for low, "Pass me this" or "Pass me that." The tin dishes clinked and steel calks crunched into the floor as the men adjusted their feet under the benches. The rain pattered monotonously. Water from the roof splashed into pools along the walls.

Rarely did anyone pay attention to strangers, for the men rarely knew each other. The only thing of interest in a newcomer was his bottle of whiskey — if he had one. No bottle of whiskey — no interest.

I squeezed into my place at the table. I was starving. I had hardly started eating when I saw a lumberjack crowding himself onto a bench. I thought at once that there was something familiar about him.

It was Ole, the bucker, the first lumberjack with whom I had become acquainted on Puget Sound. As he settled into place, Ole leveled his glance and noticed and recognized me. I nodded and smiled, but he winced as his shoulders sagged.

Ole had not gone to Sweden to see his mother as he had planned. He had been on one of his periodic sprees and he showed every effect from it. The two years since I had seen Ole had exacted a toll. His shoulders drooped more, his eyes were duller and his movements more insipid. He seemed ashamed, too. I was depressed but anxious to help. Ole had his weakness, but he was a grand guy.

After supper I went to the bunkhouse to wait for Ole. The

place felt drearier than I had ever experienced a bunkhouse except the one on the Tacoma Eastern. It was a large bunkhouse with a small crew. Nearly all the men were immigrants of several nationalities. They were sitting in little knots and speaking their native languages. The bare walls of the bunkhouse; the damp, chilled, and piercing air; the dirt-strewn floor; and the stinky vapor from drying clothes caused an atmosphere of extreme discomfort. I waited — listening to the singsong of the Swedes, the K-K-K-Ks of the Fins, and the constant striking of the rain.

Ole found his way back to the bunkhouse. He shivered from the cold and wet. He slid stiff, calloused hands down his head and face to wipe off the rain, then rubbed them over the stove.

Ole had taught me much on our journey to McDougal & Jackson's camp and while we were there, and although our interests away from camp were not in common, we had become fast friends. I walked across the bunkhouse and sat beside him. Lumberjacks are not demonstrative when they are recovering from a spree, and Ole was not only sobering, he was sick. He retched. I slipped my arm about his shoulders and we talked low. Ole had not fulfilled his desire to go to Sweden. The depression of 1907 was the cause.

The other lumberjacks spread out their dirty blankets. Only their tinpants were removed and stood against the walls, thrown onto vacant bunks, or kicked under the long deacon's seat. Ole kept his on — they were all he had. He passed into a stupor, his body increasingly sagged, his head plunged between his knees.

When I rose to leave, I glanced at Ole's turkey. There was a torn, dirty, wet quilt beside it. I had seen that quilt in a heap near a stump. The bunk held only bit of straw along the edges — not enough padding for comfort. But Ole was silent. He had experienced discomfort many times, and a regular lumberjack did not complain. Discomfort was a part of his living.

"Come on," I commanded. I pushed the filthy quilt aside and grabbed his turkey. Ole shuffled after me.

The shack that I occupied was barren and small. I had requisitioned it when the camp was reopened and, with slight repairs, had made it quite similar to the one that I had built at Mc-Dougal & Jackson's camp near Buckley. Ole and I could be alone there. I built a fire to dry Ole's clothes and I shared my bunk with him so he would be under warm blankets. Exhausted, he fell into deep sleep and sprawled there till morning.

When we awakened before daylight, Ole was fairly revived, quite cheerful, thankful, and ready to go to work. We shacked together from then on.

Ole started bucking that morning. The wages were low and the work was hard because the timber was poorly felled. He planned to stay until Christmas vacation, then go to Seattle or Tacoma or maybe Grays Harbor. Vancouver, British Columbia, had a good reputation. After New Year's he would get a real job with better wages. He would save just enough money to go to Sweden. Or he might get a job on a windjammer and earn enough money on the way or get free passage. Ole had good intentions, but he had firmly developed habits.

Although Ole was much older than I, he acted as if I were his big brother. He readily responded to suggestions while in camp. While we shacked together, he cleaned himself better and showed signs of strengthening his will. We played cribbage, and when I wrote to my grandmother on Sundays, he told me about his mother whom he would see soon. We walked together to Matlock to mail letters and to buy little things. Ole liked to buy the Police Gazette. He liked the pictures of the girls. Occasionally, we guddled steelhead trout, chasing them into tiny coves in a nearby creek and catching them with our hands. We carried the fish to the cookhouse for the crew. The steelheads were more delicious than the bony dog-salmons the company bought from fishermen in Olympia. When I went for any little stroll, Ole came along, puppy-like, and if I did anything for pleasure, he tried to take part. No argument — no objections to anything.

At first, the days at Camp E passed swiftly, or as swiftly as rainy, cold, slushy days can pass. They began to lag as Christmas neared. The men became more animated, discussing where they would go and what they would do.

The Saturday before Christmas we would leave on the railroad trucks and scatter to Seattle, Tacoma, and Everett. The lumberjacks began to clean up. They shook the dust, straw, and dirt out of their blankets and hung them on branches, old wires, pieces of haulback, or nails driven in trees, or they spread them over stumps or on the ground. Those with extra shoes cleaned them as the other joked about lady slippers. Nearly all wore their calked shoes in camp and in town.

I, too, got ready. But Ole had nothing to get ready. He was going to buy nicer used clothing in Olympia. They were good enough for a lumberjack like him. He would not see the ladies anyway.

"By yimminy, I'm going to Sweden to see my mother. This time, ya bet. I'da had enough money to go to Sweden now but for that depression," he said. "Damned that depression."

Thursday afternoon, two days before Christmas, two fallers made an undercut in a giant Douglas fir. It would be felled Friday and would probably take all day. It was an exceptionally large, beautiful fir, straight and clear of knots.

"When you hear that fir fall," said the headfaller, "that's all."

Friday morning dawned wet, snowy, and cold. The large fir tops were faintly visible. The small, stripped trees looked like sharp spears.

The Oregon mist was at its worst, and the damp snow on the ferns and shrubs melted and dripped into our shoes and our baggy, soggy leather gloves. We would be yarding our last log, and as we squeezed the water from our clothes and pressed the mud from our shoes, we called, "Merry Chirstmas!"

The crew was given orders to wind things up. All jobs started were to be finished. Yarding rigging had to be gathered and placed on the donkey sled. Even the haulback had to be pulled in, a hard job. The fallers were to turn in their saws, wedges, hammers, springboards, and oil bottles to the tool-house. The buckers had to do likewise with their tools. Yes, sir, vacation time for lumberjacks.

The day passed slowly, too slowly, and there seemed to be an unusual stillness in the air and woods. When the donkey stopped, the dripping rain and melted snow seemed to fall harder from the branches. Big drops splashed inside our clothes and made us wince. But this was the last day. Who cared about the discomfort?

At intervals we heard the fallers in the distance. We heard wedges being pounded. Silence while the fallers adjusted themselves on their springboards.

We peered through the brush. The fallers swung their axes rhythmically, then picked up their saw.

"Timber –er –er –er –er!!" The cracking wood deadened the sound of the snipping sawteeth.

The fir's branches shivered, and the top moved slowly. The giant tree shuddered.

"Timber –er –er –er –er!!"

"Let her come! Let her come –m –m –m!" commanded the buckers as the fallers jumped from their springboards and dragged their axes and the saw to safety.

The long symmetrical cone-shaped fir swung earthward, merging with the other trees. The great trunk swung and swerved. The air blasted and filled with needles, leaves, branches, moss, and dust. The surrounding firs swayed. We heard the tearing and breaking of branches as the other trees were stripped.

"Timber –er –er –er –er!"

The fir lunged and disappeared in the air. Crash! Debris swirled outward, then inward, then floated down onto the prostrate fir.

The day's work was done.

The rigging crew gathered about the donkey while the fireman emptied the firebox and splashed water over the embers, as though there could be a forest fire in such weather. The engineer put his donkey in order for the vacation. That night we were all going to camp together.

As we shuffled, talked, and looked at the fallers and the buckers climbing over logs, and circling about among the stumps and trees, we heard their subdued voices. They were not jumping or hurrying.

"Hurry, you guys," someone called in merriment. There was no response. Their forms grew more distinct, and we noticed that they were grouped closely. Slowly, as they came nearer, we saw their leaning forms and heard their low voices.

We stepped forward a little and strained to look. We glanced at each other. We were silent.

The forms emerged from the woods and staggered along the skidtrail, two ahead and one behind. They were carrying something.

We stared and we slid the water from our faces as silently the men laid their burden — a lumberjack — on the muddy ground. The rain fell on his face and spread and flowed down through his stubbled beard.

Ole was dead.

Ole had run far enough from the falling fir, but the burst of air dislodged a widowmaker. It fell and crushed him.

Sorrowfully, we laid my pal upon a logging truck and pushed it to camp. On the way I shed some tears that mixed with the rain.

That night, Ole, the Swede, the bucker, lay in the tool house where the woodrats jumped and sneaked and snooped.

We were subdued that night. In the cookhouse, the bunkhouse, the office, there were only whispers and hushed movements. "Poor devil."

Saturday forenoon dragged, and as noon approached, the crew began to drift to camp and carried their tools to the tool house.

Dinner — then pay.

"How much did I get? Oh, not so much."

Washing and packing. Some shaving.

Silently and singly, the men went to the tool house. They tiptoed their calked shoes on the floor and raised a corner of the new blanket — a gift from the company — to look at Ole.

Dinner — wait. Long dragging minutes. Late that after-noon, the Mason County coroner arrived to conduct an au-topsy. Death by accident. Filling a few blanks on a paper. Not much concern. Official business.

After the autopsy, several linked railroad trucks were backed to the platform of the toolshed and on one of them a space was cleared. Tenderly — as tenderly as a laborer's cal-loused hands can be tender — four lumberjacks folded the blanket about the body and carried it to the truck.

In my shack I had put my chum's few effects in his turkey. Among the dirty things were a few soiled and wrinkled letters written in Swedish. No one but I saw them. Carefully tucked between the pages of one letter was a frayed and fingered pic-ture of an old lady with a motherly smile.

And, through my tears, as I saw that dear face, vividly I saw another old lady, an old lady whom I adored and longed to see.

I was the last one of the crew to leave that truck when we arrived at the landing where we would catch a tug to Olympia. As I passed the body, I raised a corner of the blanket to give my friend a last look of farewell, then I jumped aboard the tug and turned away.

The engine blew its raucous whistle, the paddles splashed, and the tug scooted out. Behind on the dock stood the coroner of Mason County, waiting for the next passing boat that would take him and Ole's remains to Shelton and the potter's field. The tug floated out into a narrow strait, then around a point.

I did not return to Camp E.

CHAPTER 19

Driving Logs on the Lewis River

E ARLY IN THE SPRING OF **1909** I worked a few weeks in a logging camp about five hundred miles north of Vancouver, British Columbia. The rocky, steep coastal terrain and inferior equipment of loggers who tried to imitate Puget Sound methods made hooktending difficult. I soon returned to Seattle.

There I learned that Joe Beledeau, who had been superintendent when I worked for S. E. Slade Lumber Company, was superintendent of some logging camps on upper Lewis River. I decided to take a chance on getting a job by merely showing up at the camp. On the way, I stopped at Woodland where I deposited my money, about two hundred dollars.

I was told that if I walked on the good road that ran along the river, someone would soon give me a ride. The day was warm, and my turkey was filled with winter clothes. I soon tired. But I had not gone far when a rancher with a team and wagon overtook me and invited me to ride with him. The seat with the springs was delightful.

There was another man on the wagon, a businessman, it seemed to me. As we rode, we told each other our occupations.

"My name's Albert Miller," the man said, extending his hand. He was president, manager, and principal owner of the Lewis River Boom Company.

The Lewis River Boom Company did not cut timber. It drove logs for the logging companies, sorting and rafting them at the boom[48] where the Lewis River flowed into the Columbia River.

Albert Miller — he would not let me call him mister — impressed me with his friendliness, so when he offered me a job as rigging-slinger with his driving crew, I accepted. The job paid two dollars and board per day, and we worked every day, including Sundays.

Except in one stretch where the two rivers merged, Lewis River was narrow and shallow. The logs floated well only during freshets caused by the seasonal melting of snow in the mountains.

Nearly all the timber cut along the Lewis River was red fir, and the logs were not as large as those cut around Grays Harbor and Puget Sound. They were more uniform, from one to three feet in diameter and no more than twenty-four feet long. There was some cedar, but it was not important.

I had driven pine logs on the Peshekee River in the Huron Mountains in Michigan but driving logs on the Lewis River was different. They were too large, long, and heavy to be moved

---

[48] *A log boom is a barrier placed in a river designed to collect and contain floating logs so they could be sorted by owner or towed like a raft to a mill.*

Example of a river scow with some of the features described by the author. (Courtesy of the Mendocino Historical Society.)

with peaveys. When they became stranded, they were dislodged with machinery. During low water, they had to be pulled over numerous riffles and small rapids.

Our job consisted only of driving logs — we had nothing to do with the booming and rafting. Our equipment included a small, two-drum, double-geared yarder of the latest type. For transportation, we had a small, flat-bottomed rowboat and a scow with a large stern paddlewheel.

Logging donkeys on land are set on heavy sleds made of timber. Our river donkey was set on the beams of the clumsy scow. The scow was about thirty feet long and ten feet wide. The bottom was rounded at each end so we could move it forward or backward. At the front was a piledriver tower about twenty feet high and weighing about one thousand pounds. The piledriver was used to drive piles to make small levies to close off little coves where logs sometimes drifted. It was also used to make breakwaters in bends where the current washed the banks and to drive the big piles that held the booms at the mouth of the river.

The roof over the donkey extended back to cover a little cabin, which included a small wood stove, a table on hinges fastened to the wall, and a box for food and dishes. The cook hung his utensils along the wall.

In the back of the cabin there were two tiers of double bunks. Whenever we remained anchored at a place for more than one day, we pitched a tent on the bank, and in clear weather the cook did his cooking over an open fire. The board was very good.

When we worked a good distance up the river from Woodland, our meat was salted and smoked. We bought eggs, vegetables, and fruit from the ranchers. The fruit that we liked best were the blackberries, strawberries, and raspberries. When plums and Royal Ann and Black Republican cherries were ripening, the ranchers invited us to help ourselves.

Moving the scow was quite an undertaking. On the upper part of the river the paddlewheel was useless — the water was too shallow and the current too swift. When it scraped the river bottom, we fastened the main line to a stump or tree, and the donkey was powerful enough to pull itself.

Only during the periodic high waters of summer could we predict the rise in the current of the Lewis River. At times we would go to bed while the water was so low that logs could not float, and frequently, before the night had passed, the scow had floated free. The logs darted, bumped, and jammed down the stream. Some rolled up the bank.

It was during one of those freshets that I woke one morning and saw a strange sight. On the surface of the water I saw floating countless gray objects, some were tiny, and others were about the size of a baseball. I reached over the scow and intercepted several. They were circular but flat on top and bottom. They felt hard like rock. I could not believe that rocks were floating on water. The foreman told me that they were porous pumice stones, probably from Mount St. Helens. After a few hours, the pumice stones became saturated, and when the water receded, there were many on the banks.

On some of the ranches along the river there were small scattered cedars that the owners cut into short logs, usually eight feet long, and sold at the mouth of the Lewis River. They were loaded onto scows and shipped to shingle mills, usually in Portland.

To transport their cedar logs, the ranchers bound them into rafts and guided them with long poles. On one occasion while we were anchored at the foot of a little rapid, we saw two ranchers riding a raft of cedar logs on a calm pool. On the raft there were two small valises. The ranchers planned to drive the logs to a boom, then board a boat to Portland.

As the raft accelerated and neared the rapid, the current slashed the rear against the end of some logs. The raft tore apart, and the cedar logs scattered. The ranchers lost their valises as, with difficulty, they pulled themselves onto the jam of logs and staggered to the bank. The owners of the land along the banks later gathered the logs into rafts of their own.

One of the men who worked with us was Mat O'Connor, whose home was in Portland. He had worked in the salmon canneries of Astoria and knew much about catching salmon in the Columbia River. He knew how to cook shad roe that the rowboat fishermen gave us, and he was a sportsman in preparing the juicy red salmon sides.

Mat described the salmon traps and the salmon ladders further up the river. He related how he had caught five- and six-foot sturgeon when they were plentiful and before there were legal restrictions on them. By 1909, sturgeon could be caught only during certain short periods. But Mat knew how to beat the legal restrictions — by poaching.

One day while we were examining logs in the coves and bayous in the north bank of the Columbia River, I learned how to handle poached sturgeon. We were jumping from log to log, examining the brands on the ends, when I noticed rhythmic splashes in the water. In the deepest water, I could see the top of a stake.

"A sturgeon!" I shouted, pleased and surprised, for I had

heard so much about staking sturgeon.

We all hopped to the scene. Only Mat had ever seen a staked sturgeon.

"That's one," he said, sidling up to the stake. He pointed out that the stake was made of clothesline.

To circumvent the conservation law that restricted the extensive catching of sturgeons that were rapidly becoming extinct, poachers caught sturgeons before the season opened, bridled them, then anchored them to a stake in some obscure bayou. There was an unwritten understanding among poachers to let each other's catch alone.

To stake a sturgeon, a small, strong stick, about eight inches long was tied at the middle by a rope or wire that passed through its mouth and gill.

Sometimes boys and uncooperating poachers traveled up and down the river stealing staked sturgeons and re-staking them in other bayous. "Be on your way," was an admonition to anyone who was suspected of snooping.

After admiring the setup, we were on our way, too.

When the Columbia River rose and flooded the banks of the valley, the Lewis River backed up and rose so high, it sometimes went over the tops of the boom piles. At those times, the booms could not hold all the logs, so many of them went out of control and floated into the Columbia River where some were intercepted by men living along the banks. Those men would tow the logs into coves and bayous near their homes and assemble them into small rafts. They sawed off the ends of the logs to destroy the logging companies' brands and sold the logs. If they did not remove the brands, they would surrender them to the boom companies at exorbitant prices.

In the summer of 1909, the water at the boom of the Lewis River rose unusually high and many fine logs floated into the current of the Columbia River. After the water had receded, we were ordered to go along the riverbank in a tug to retrieve those logs. Several small coves jutting into the north bank of the Columbia River were filled with logs, some of which bore the brands that must have belonged to loggers further west than the Lewis River. The ends of some of the logs had been sawed, which was a clear indication that they had been poached. The foreman readily recognized some brands as belonging to companies whose logs we were driving. There were other coves and little piers to which rafts were tied on the other side of the river, so we pulled out to explore the south bank of the Columbia River.

We crossed the swift current and reached the opposite bank at a tiny wharf at Columbia City where we saw a raft of logs.

Columbia City was one of the first settlements established on the west side of the river. However nice the settlement had been, by 1909 it consisted of a small frame house, outhouse, and other small buildings. They were all unpainted and sagging.

Mat O'Connor steered the tug to the side of the raft and

sprang on the logs and started to tie up at one of the piles. Frank Miller stepped off with him. The two men had hardly set foot on the logs or knotted the hawser when out of the house came two roughly dressed men, one middle aged and the other younger — probably father and son. An unkempt, beefy woman stood akimbo near the door. Each man carried a rifle and strode briskly toward the wharf.

"Don't tie that rope and get off my raft," commanded the older man sternly as he swung his rifle to rest in the crook of his arm.

Frank Miller stepped on the end of a log. He recognized the brand as belonging to one of the companies whose logs we drove.

"I'll pay you," Frank suggested, smiling.

I held my breath. Frank and Mat stepped off the raft. Tense silence.

"I said get off those logs," said the older man as he strode toward the mooring rope, fingering the trigger of his rifle. Before he could reach the rope, Mat flung it out of the man's reach, and he and Frank leaped to the tug and shoved it away from the pile.

Mat struggled frantically to point the tug up stream while the rest of the crew watched the residents of Columbia City standing fixed until we were enveloped in the dusk.

Two or three days after the Columbia City episode, we started up the Lewis River. I had worked the river for four months, but the water was getting too cold. When we got to Woodland, I quit and went to Aberdeen.

CHAPTER 20

On the Wishkah River

HAYNES & PRESTON WERE CONTRACTORS who had the reputation of always having owned and maintained the most up-to-date equipment for logging. They owned two powerful yarders, and their rigging was the best.

The area they were logging was a short distance up the East Fork of the Wishkah River, about eight miles north of Aberdeen. The Wishkah River flows south into Grays Harbor.

The river's main run was large enough to float logs all year; however, the East Fork was short, and its crooked course flowed down a narrow valley. The bends were sharp enough to make driving logs difficult when the water was low, but the banks were steep, so when the water was high, large logs could be floated.

A short way up the East Fork was an old, well-constructed log dam that was still useful. When the gate was closed, the marsh above it became a pond to hold the logs in a boom, after which they could be sluiced[49] and released into the main stream.

---

[49] *A sluice is an artificial water channel, often made of wood, controlled at its head by a gate. Built on hillsides, they were used to move logs quickly downhill.*

Nearly all of the timber was on the narrow and level swamp bottom along the East Fork and averaged quite large. It included many unusually fine spruces and cedars, as well as some excellent firs.

Quite a few large trees in the swamp had been felled and bucked many years before. Some had become thoroughly water-soaked deadheads.[50] The water had never been deep enough to float them, and oxen were not strong enough to yard them. Haynes & Preston could have built a skidroad along the foot of one ridge and dragged the logs to the pond above the dam, but they chose to gamble on floating them to the dam, because they had two powerful donkeys that could dislodge them if they became stuck.

The dam on the East Fork of the Wishkah was not too far from salt water. Although the water was usually shallow and swirling in the sluice, many beautiful salmon swam through during their runs. The unusually large ones sometimes became stranded on the timber bottom of the sluice. During the runs, the cook visited the dam nearly every day and speared enough fish for the crew. He fed us what he said were the best portions, the bellies and sides. Sunday afternoons I helped him spear many salmon. It was not sport — it was like spearing fish in a tub.

Late in November 1909, nearly all the logs had been yarded and piled high between the banks of the river. As we advanced up the river, we inquired about the number of logs

---

[50] *Previously felled, submerged timber.*

that remained to be yarded. We could yard twenty-five to forty a day. All the fellows were real lumberjacks, skilled and enthusiastic about their work. Nearly every man who had started in the camp stayed to the last. The food was the best, the wages were adequate and the expert workmanship made the work as pleasant as logging could be.

One evening, the foreman told us that he had just counted the remaining logs. There were one hundred and ninety-eight to yard. Just a few more days of yarding. The foreman was nervous, but the members of the firm were optimistic. The Oregon mist had begun to thicken for the winter and every increase in rain buoyed their spirits. We all watched diligently for the rising water.

A few logs left to yard — then what? If the water rose but did not float the logs away, mud and silt would settle among them, damming the river, and erosion would create a new channel. The logs would be bypassed. That had happened to much timber in other rivers with disastrous financial results.

Thanksgiving was only a few days off, and we were beginning to talk of Christmas vacation.

Jim Preston went to Aberdeen two days before Thanksgiving to get supplies. The day before Thanksgiving was like nearly all the other days of that season — it rained as it can rain in the Grays Harbor region. We came in from work while it was raining, we spent the evening while it was raining, we bunked to the sound of the rain.

The wind increased as the night progressed. We had to work in the rain, or else we did not work, but the wind was different. The snags with their bare roots, and the conky trunks might break, and the tops of the trees might topple on us. Those damned widowmakers.

"Looks like a day off," fellows said.

As the night wore on, more of the crew began to wake and to talk louder and louder. Every time someone opened the door to check the weather, we saw by the faint light of a small oil lamp the myriad streaks of driving rain. Men went back and forth to the door to watch the rain. If the rain could only last long enough to flood the stream. For once we wanted rain badly.

Someone mentioned the little dam just below the marsh. Its gate should be closed. Was it closed?

Frantically, some of us jammed ourselves into our wet shirts, tinpants, and soggy calked shoes. We scrambled down the muddy, deep-rutted road along the edge of the marsh to the dam. We let down the gate into the rising current, then sloshed to the bunkhouse to get out of that cold rain and away from the invisible, but ever-present snags and the widowmakers.

Water rises fast in those narrow valleys. Somebody opened the door; the water was shining in the marsh. Suddenly there was a thump. Was it an uprooted tree striking another tree? More thumps. We glanced at each other. Too many thumps at short intervals for uprooted trees.

A fellow opened the door and stepped out on the little covered porch. Nothing visible but the darts of rain, but the thumps were louder and more frequent. The wind howled. Dark, pitch dark.

"What time?"

"Three o'clock, about."

"Four o'clock, about."

The thumps increased.

The foreman, Ben Cooksey, crunched his calked shoes down the steps into the mud. The sky over the long ridge was beginning to lighten. He climbed back — excited and pleased.

We waited for daylight. The thumping continued.

The water became more visible. Things took form — logs, dimly lit, floated from the edges of the river and down the current, thumping into each other.

In the bitter discomfort of the rain, and the danger from falling snags and trees and widowmakers, we worked all day. We had to work hard and fast. Water in a stream such as the East Fork recedes rapidly. Into the night we worked as we groped our way about and into increasing danger. And we did it. We drove all those logs down into the pond where they pressed against the dam.

Jim Preston was an appreciative man. Thanksgiving Day was pleasant. Early that morning we were invited to the wonagon where each lumberjack received a gift of a new outfit of work clothes. The day was damp and chilly, but the cookhouse and the bunkhouse were warm. We played cards, reminisced, and told stories animated by the coming vacation.

Dinner and supper were lavish. Thanksgiving dinner had all the trimmings along with a large keg of beer and plenty of whiskey. What a celebration for lumberjacks!

Only a few men stayed in camp to sluice the logs through the dam into the stream below. We were through with the East Fork of the Wishkah River. And so were Haynes & Preston as loggers. They had gambled — an honest gamble — and they had made a fortune.

CHAPTER 21

End of the Road

WORKING IN THE LOGGING CAMPS was exhausting. The initial enthusiasm of working on Puget Sound and Grays Harbor soon wore off. One quit voluntarily or was forced from it through necessity. The high wages caused by the San Francisco fire never fully recovered after the financial panic of 1907. And although wages had increased some in the fall of 1908, they began to sag again in 1910. The attractive jobs became fewer and fewer. Most of the timber on the level and slightly rolling ground was gone, and the larger logging companies with the modern and powerful equipment were moving into rugged mountain terrain. High-lead logging was starting.[51]

The loggers with worn and outdated equipment struggled to survive by salvaging hemlock, spruce, cedar, and large snags and windfalls that were scattered among the debris of bygone days and new growth.

During spring I had worked in two log salvaging camps,

---

[51] *High-lead logging combined the power of steam donkeys with a system of cables and blocks rigged overhead among the trees. It increased the pace of logging and made it possible to harvest trees in formerly inaccessible areas.*

one on the bank of Green Lake near Seattle and the other near Orting. Tending hook in such camps was depressingly hard. The competition among skilled lumberjacks for the better paying jobs was keen and the physical requirements more exacting. In the better camps, only the sturdiest young men could be hooktenders or loaders, for the rugged ground with the necessary heavier equipment sapped strength in a very few years.

By July 4, 1910, I had been logging a few weeks more than four years. I was twenty-four and exhausting fast. I decided to get out by next Christmas, but fate had other plans for me.

I headed to Seattle for the 4th of July vacation.

I always enjoyed visiting the Seattle waterfront. There was life in all of its ramifications — an excellent education in human nature. One could see everything from the filthiest harbor rat salvaging in the slimy water to the construction of the United States battleship *Nebraska*.

The employment offices were jammed more than ever. Railroad construction was waning. More men and fewer jobs.

I became convinced of the futility of continuing to work in the logging camps. A last spurt at fair wages would augment my savings enough for me to begin my life's project, but where were the jobs at fair wages?

"Hello, Bill," said a familiar voice. It was Red Campbell.

We had been hooktenders for S.E. Slade Lumber Company when that firm operated two sides near Elma in 1907.

"Balcom & Vanderhoof up near Hartford wants a loader,"

Red said. "The work's damned hard, but the pay is okay. You can get five bucks and board. Come on."

So, the work was hard. Where was it not hard?

The next Sunday afternoon, Red and I went to Everett and then to Hartford.

The camp buildings had been constructed to house a crew for three sides, but the operation now had only one side. The bunkhouse was in a bad state of disrepair and too large for the small crew. It was littered with all sorts of rubbish — old blankets, quilts that had been thrown out and then carried in again, shoes, and sour old clothes. Worn tools and machinery lay about outside.

Crew members were constantly leaving and new ones coming. They were unusually inefficient, and many could not speak English. Red Campbell, the locomotive engineer, and the foreman were the only lumberjacks who could be classified as steady. Hartford was near Everett and Seattle, so it was easy for tramp workers to find the camp, earn a few dollars, then quit. They were not lumberjacks, they were drifters. The camp's one good feature was the fine quality of the food, an indispensable requirement for keeping even a makeshift crew.

The terrain being logged was considered level for logging. None of the slopes were steep enough to permit the logs to slide freely when the yarding was downhill. The low ground was so flat that after the rainy season set in, the surface was always flooded, and the logs churned it into mud. The underbrush was thick, and as the logs, nearly all large spruce and cedar, were dragged, they pulled along tangled spring-maples, broken branches, small trees, and stumps. Such terrain and debris were not so bad during dry weather, but all that changed with the rainy season.

The logs were yarded directly to a landing because the railroad was constructed into the timber, making skidroads unnecessary. The landings were level with the rails, and they were never long enough for two rows of logs, which would have helped in sorting them.

A landing was not used for long before the spaces between the skids were filled with clay mixed with debris. We went to work wet and muddy, and we slopped in the mud all day. We lived in mud.

Only the fair wages and knowing I would be quitting kept me at Balcom & Vanderhoof's. I had a calendar in my timebook and each night, like a miser counting his hoard, I counted the days — days that were cold, dreary, and exhausting, days that increasingly taxed my endurance. They were short days in hours but long in work.

December 10, 1910, was no different from other rainy days of the season. The night of the ninth I had gone to bed wet. Morning came — an ineffective fire, breakfast, long waiting. At my bunk, I examined my things, waiting for daylight. They were not clothing anymore. Just things. Tinpants worn thin and cracked and frayed in the seams and folds, shoes with missing calks, slit gloves, frayed blue flannel shirt caked with mud. I had not been wearing a hat because the rain seeped through it, but there it was — shapeless.

Ten days to go. Would my clothes last?

"Well, Bill," said Red as we hopped over the railroad ties, "be going to college soon, eh?" There was a sneering expression to the remark.

"I'll go with you," added Jack Smith, the yarding donkey engineer.

There was more kidding to which I did not reply. What was the use? Those fellows would have to be shown.

At the landing, the fireman already had a full head of steam in the boiler. Red lines glowed around the edge of the firebox door. It's warmth was so inviting. Water spouted from the dilapidated roof. We stepped from the mud onto the donkey sled and stretched our arms to warm our numb hands. As the swamp grew lighter, I saw the narrow streaks of water in the deep skid trails, the shiny gray mud on the landing, and the treacherous spring-maples ready to be released.

Red and his crew got to work, fighting logs through the debris down to the skidtrails, down to the swamp, and into the little canals where the chokered logs hooked the spring-maples, broke branches and roots, plowed through mud, and dumped a flood of water onto the landing. The hooktender and his men waved and shouted. We cursed as each log pushed us off of our feet. The chaser waded through, damning everything.

The first log was a spruce butt about five feet in diameter at the stump end. It was churn-butted and the large end was somewhat lopsided. Such a log required careful rolling and sliding — it took great power. I stretched the load line over the car while the spooltender flopped the loadline to remove the kinks. I looped the loadline over the log, and the secondloader locked it to the snapline. The spooltender wrapped his line around the spool several times. Jack Smith opened the donkey's throttle.

The log rolled slowly. It hesitated as I held my hands closer and closer together, ready to snap my arms to signal. Suddenly, the log flopped against the side of the car. Now it was necessary to either roll the log or slide the other end.

We tried to roll it, but it would not slip, so I unhooked the snapline and re-hooked the bullhook to the roadline, then flopped the loop of the snapline over the small end of the log and hooked it over the side of the car that was nearest to the donkey. I stood across the donkey from the engineer where we could see each other and the log.

Jack Smith slowly raised his throttle. The loadline tightened. The log slid slightly, then jerked. Jack raised the throttle a bit more.

The ginpole leaned toward us and the guyline tightened and zinged. The log stuck fast, then a bit more steam. The log slid — stuck. More steam and then a pause.

SNAP!

The loadline flew, the ginpole swung, the guyline back-flapped. The engineer jammed his throttle and threw his arm across his eyes.

The spooltender ducked. Pieces of the loading block sailed through the air. Some fell on the car, some shot into the mud. The heavy block strap swished.

When I lowered my arms, I saw the sheave and the shell of the loading block near the log it had struck.

Aghast, we all looked at each other.

"Came near not going to Michigan that time," blurted Jack Smith.

I looked at Jack and swore.

Picking up the spare loading block, I swung it over my shoulder, as only an experienced rigging-man could do, and carried it to the foot of the ginpole. I climbed the ginpole and pulled the block up.

The loadline was repositioned, but this time I stepped back a little further than before. Jack Smith opened the throttle slightly as the spooltender pulled the loadline. The loadline tightened and slipped, tightened and slipped, and tightened again. The guyline grew tauter and tauter. The log rolled a little, stopped, then jerked sideways. Jack Smith looked apprehensive. The secondloader raised his arms, ready to jam them over his face. The spooltender took a firm hold on the loadline.

Jack Smith watched my uplifted hands. The car tipped a bit. A little more steam — more pressure on the spool....

SNAP!

The frayed ends of the ginpole block strap flew. The log flopped back. The ginpole swung. Jack jammed the throttle. Whirling, he threw his arms to his face.

The spooltender ducked as the loadline whipped the air.

A great splash of mud plastered me.

"There!" cried Jack. "Look by your feet!"

Near my feet in an ink-black hole filling with water, the block's hook pointed up.

"Where's the block?" asked the secondloader. He was pale.

I pointed to the hole and we both grimaced.

"Come near not going to college that time," said Jack.

Without hesitation, I sloshed to the donkey sled, climbed on a runner, unhooked my double-breasted muddy blue woolen shirt from a nail under the roof, and slapped it over my shoulder. I pulled off my worn, seeping gloves and threw them into the swamp.

"I'm going and I'm going right now." There was not much left for me to say. I was through, physically and mentally.

I shook hands with Jack Smith and the rest of the crew. I waved to Red Campbell and his crew who had seen the near fatal accident.

"See you in college," Red called.

With great relief I was on my way to Hartford, Everett, then Seattle. The afternoon of December 12, 1910, I boarded a passenger train of the newly completed extension of the Chicago, Milwaukee, St. Paul & Pacific Railroad for the east.

After many years I sometimes wonder if all that mud has ever finally seeped from my skin.

Epilogue

WILFRED REALIZED HIS DREAM OF COLLEGE, eventually earning four degrees. But for the remainder of his life, he exhibited the same mixture of restlessness, industry, and disdain that he conveyed in his account of his years on Puget Sound.

In the winter of 1911, he enrolled in Northern State Normal School (now Northern Michigan University) in Marquette. After he graduated, he taught at a one-room school in what is now Rousseau, Michigan. In 1913, he was a grade school principal in Glendive, Montana, and in 1914–1916, principal of a consolidated school in Deering, North Dakota. His summers were spent in summer school, or doing hard labor on a farm, factory, or mine.

In 1916, he enrolled at the University of Michigan, waiting tables to earn his board. He graduated in 1918 with a bachelor's degree and began taking courses toward a master's. By this time, he was in his early thirties. He met Ethel Eldred in a psychology class, and they married on August 27, 1918. He spent that summer as principal of a Charlotte, Michigan, high school.

His wife's widowed mother, Emma Eldred, owned a farm in Belmont, Michigan. In 1919, he and Ethel took over running the farm. He describes the venture as "unprofitable and unpleasant." "Unpleasant," perhaps, because his mother-in-law disliked him so much, she wrote her daughter (her only child) out of her will. (This effort was futile. After her death in 1924, Ethel and Wilfred contested the will, and the issue was settled in their favor in 1926.)

In 1920, after his first child, Lorraine, was born, he bought a farm near Caledonia, but with the panic of 1920, that farm, too, was unprofitable.

After selling the farm, Wilfred took a position as principal of a high school in Venice, Illinois. His second child, Eileen, was born in 1922, after which they moved to Persia, Iowa, where he was principal of a consolidated school. The school board, he writes, was "composed of illiterate men with whom I could not get along."

His daughter Vivian was born in 1923. He quit the school and moved to Ann Arbor where he received a master's degree from the University of Michigan.

From 1924 to 1927, he taught in a high school in Richmond, Indiana, and began to study law at the University of Michigan. His son Paul was born in 1925. He was admitted the bar on November 5, 1927.

He took a job as deputy prosecutor in Richmond, and was elected to the school board in 1929. Some of Richmond's citizens objected to a deputy prosecutor taking a position on the school board and forced him to make a choice. He choose the school board and opened his own law practice in 1929.

There is some evidence that this endeavor, too, failed, and he worked in a factory during World War II. After he retired, he spent his last years writing about logging, mining, and growing up in the Upper Peninsula. He died of a heart attack in a nursing home in River Forest, Illinois, on April 8, 1966, just shy of his eightieth birthday.

Glossary

BARKER. The lumberjack who removed the bark from the flattest side of a fir log to make it slide more easily. The flattest surface of the log was called the belly.

BLACKSMITH. Repaired camp equipment, built donkey sleds, and made chokers, choker-hooks, and other small equipment.

BLOCK. All-steel pulleys used in logging.

BUCKER. A lumberjack who worked alone while sawing trees into logs.

BULLBLOCK. A large block, or pulley, weighing one hundred to two hundred pounds. It consisted of top and bottom, steel, pear-shaped plates, the small ends of which were held by a steel gooseneck. It was anchored as low as possible to a large stump or tree by a heavy cable strap a short distance in front of the yarder or swing donkey. The bullblock made it possible to unhook the snapper from the choker on a log, pull the snapper back, and rehook it to the choker. The purpose of the block was to avoid having to open it when the heavy connecting links and swivel passed through it.

BULLCOOK. One who does caretaking jobs in a logging camp, especially helping the cook.

BULLHOOK. A hook for attaching chokers to a line.

CALK SHOES. Caulk shoes or boots have steel spikes protruding from the bottom of the sole for traction.

CANTHOOK. A tool consisting of a long, wooden handle with an iron hook at one end.

CHOKER. A length of cable that encircled the end of a log so the log could be pulled. The harder the yarder pulled, the tighter the choker became, hence its name.

CHOKERMAN. The man who set the chokers around the logs where they lay in the woods.

CHASER. The man who followed the log after the rigging-slinger had started it on its way to the yarder. At the yarder, he removed the choker and ordered the choker and line to be pulled back (originally by horse, but after 1907, by steam donkey) to the woods for another log.

CONK. A white fungus on fir trees. It caused the wood to decay above and below it. The result was a thick layer of dark rot. Conks burned readily when they were dry and made extinguishing forest fires difficult.

COUPLINGS. Two pairs of large steel hooks. Each pair was connected to a piece of cable and was used to join logs into turns.

CRIBBING. A timber structure used to support heavy objects, such as railroad tracks.

DOGGER. The lumberjack who coupled logs into turns.

DONKEY. Steam-powered winches used in handling logs. (The term derives from sailing ships where donkeys were used for loading and unloading cargo or raising large sails.) There were two distinct models, and each model came in various sizes. The roader could be used as a yarder, but the yarder could not be used as a roader. On land, all donkeys were bolted on top of large wooden sleds, and each pulled itself wherever it was needed. The types of donkeys were yarder, roader, loaders, scow, swing, and snub. For the principal uses of these engines, see their names in this glossary.

FALLER. One of a pair of men who worked together to fell trees. The headfaller had charge of all the technical details, and the secondfaller helped him by carrying tools, clearing away the brush, and other tasks.

GINPOLE. A stout upright pole, or small log, with one end resting on the ground. The top of the ginpole leaned slightly over the flatcar and was held in place by three guylines. At the top of the log hung a pulley or block through which the loading-line passed.

HAULBACK. A long, steel cable more than double the length of the main or yardline. For yarding, it pulled the yardline back to the logs where they lay in the woods; however, for a roader it pulled the roadline back up the skidroad. The haulback ran through haulback blocks.

HAULBACK BLOCK. A thin steel pulley anchored to a tree or stump as high as a man could reach. The haulback line passed through it.

HOOKTENDER. Boss of the yarding crew. He had charge of moving and setting the yarder, setting the haulback, and engineering the yarding of the logs.

LOAD DONKEY. A steam winch used to load logs onto flatcars or railroad trucks.

LOADERS. Men who loaded logs onto flatcars or railroad trucks.

LOADLINE. A cable used to load logs.

PEAVEY. Like a canthook but with the addition of a pointed metal tip.

PIGBOAT. A flat-bottomed sled about three or four inches high and pointed at both ends. It was fastened onto the tail log of a turn and used to carry small equipment down the skidroad. A road haulback pulled the pigboat back up the skidroad to its starting point.

PIKEPOLE. A long-handled tool for moving logs on water, similar to a peavey.

PITCH. A thick, sticky substance between seams in the lower part of a fir, sometimes extending many feet up. In fluid form, it is reddish yellow; but if thick, it can be almost white. It hardens when it dries in the wood.

RIGGING-SLINGER. The hooktender's helper. Directed and helped the chokermen, hooked the snapper onto the choker, and had charge of the yarding when the hooktender was otherwise occupied.

ROAD DONKEY. A steam winch used to pull logs from the yarder over skidroads to a landing.

SAWFILER. A man whose job it was to keep the saws sharpened.

SCISSORBILL. A showoff, an eastern lumberjack.

SCOW DONKEY. A steam winch installed on a scow for use on water when driving logs.

SETTING. The area logged off by a yarder.

SIDE. A complete crew and equipment connected with a one-yarder outfit and the area logged in a setting.

SIGNALPUNK. Gave signals between a working crew in the timber or along a skidroad to the engineer on a donkey. When in sight of both, the signalpunk signaled by hand; otherwise, he signaled by means of a wire attached to a whistle on the donkey.

SKIDROAD CHASER. He had charge of the turns from the yarder to the landing or to the road donkey. He removed the couplings from the turn, loaded them onto the pigboat and took them back for the next turn. He road on the pigboat like a surfer.

SKIDROAD. A road made of stout logs set either perpendicular to the direction of the road (a cross skid) or in the same direction (a fore-an-aft) over which logs were dragged for long distances.

SNAPLINE. A length of cable no longer than fifty feet that was used to reach from the snapper to the choker. It was also used to manipulate logs around stumps.

SNAPPER. A short length of cable attached to a strong swivel and links that connected the main cable to the haulback. At one end it had a hook to fasten to the choker.

SNIPE. The rounded front end of a log which allowed the log to glance off stumps and other objects and prevented it from gouging the ground when it was dragged.

SNIPER. A lumberjack who chopped the snipe.

SNUB DONKEY. A steam winch with a larger brake than a road donkey used to prevent turns from sliding out of control down a steep grade on a skidroad.

SPOOL. A steel spool used to load logs or pull objects. About a foot long and eight inches in diameter at the ends, it was fastened to the end of a drum shaft on the donkey. The loadline was wrapped around the spool as many times as needed. When the spooltender pulled the line it tightened on the spool. The loose cable piled up behind the spooltender who had to unwind the cable by flopping it round and round, like a cowboy unwinding his lariat.

SPOOLTENDER. Handled the loadline used on a spool for loading logs.

SPRINGBOARD. A hardwood board from six to eight inches wide and about four feet long. A steel plate was bolted to one end of the board and the edge of the plate bent up to hold the springboard in place. The sharp end of the plate was inserted into a notch in the base of a tree above the roots. The two fallers stood on a springboard to cut the tree.

SPRING-MAPLE. Small, slender maples that bent easily under the weight of fallen trees and which were dangerous when struck by an ax, because they could spring up unexpectedly.

SWAMPER. A man who cleared away brush and trimmed branches from logs.

SWING DONKEY. A steam winch used to pull logs from the yarder to a skidroad.

TURN. Six to ten logs coupled end to end so they can be hauled over skidroads.

WEDGES. Long, thin, broad, steel wedges inserted into saw cuts during felling to prevent the wood from closing on the saw. Also used to force trees off balance.

WHISTLEWIRE. A long wire (usually a telephone wire) that the signalpunk extended from a donkey whistle into the woods to give signals to a donkey engineer. Signals:

- One whistle: Pull
- One whistle: Stop pulling
- Two whistles: Pull on the haulback
- Three whistles: Pull slowly and hold

WINDFALL. Usually a dead tree the wind had blown down.

WIDOWMAKER. Broken branches and dry knots hanging in trees.

YARD DONKEY. A steam winch used to pull logs from where they had been cut.

YARDLINE. A steel cable used to drag logs.